T0208211

THE CALL TO ARMS

The Battle for the Hearts, Minds, and Souls of Men

STEPHEN ALLEN NEWBY

WESTBOW
PRESS®
A DIVISION OF THOMAS NELSON
& ZONDERVAN

WestBow Press books may be ordered through booksellers or by contacting:

WestBow Press
A Division of Thomas Nelson & Zondervan
1663 Liberty Drive
Bloomington, IN 47403
www.westbowpress.com
1 (866) 928-1240

ISBN: 978-1-9736-5881-8 (sc)
ISBN: 978-1-9736-5880-1 (e)

Library of Congress Control Number: 2019904060

Print information available on the last page.

WestBow Press rev. date: 04/22/2019

Religious / Christian Life / Men's Issues
Religious / Christian Life / Spiritual Growth

About the Book

The Call to Arm's premise is this: The moment we give our hearts and lives to Jesus Christ we are enrolled into spiritual battle. The unholy trinity (the world, the flesh, and the devil) wars against us daily. This book honestly confronts the challenges and struggles all Christian men know and face.

This book notes that many men have gone AWOL in their day to day walk with Jesus Christ. It takes an honest look at some of the things that call out to us; the very assaults the enemy uses to thwart our love and obedience to the call of God in our lives.

Our need for renewal via the Word of God is stressed; that we might overwrite the corrupt database within us; within our hearts.

The Call to Arms examines what the Word of God says about both the heart and mind of a man. 1 Corinthians 16:13 encourages us with these words: "Be on the alert, stand firm in the faith, act like men, be strong."

Sections speak on the pain and brokenness of divorce, of loneliness, and of the father wound; areas of woundedness within us and the beauty of brokenness these trials bring into our lives.

There's a straightforward look at the power of our words and what it means to be a true man in our thoughts, words, and deeds.

God is our Supreme Commander in this battle we are called into. Qualities and attributes of God are scripturally addressed, as well as our role as watchmen under His command. <u>The Call to Arms</u> speaks of our need to re-enlist into His service.

Additionally, there is a 5-day study guide at the end of each chapter to deepen our understanding of both the material we read and about ourselves.

About the Author

Nothing moves the heart of Steve more than a changed life. He has experienced just that in his. He has a love for the Lord and for people, especially for children, and a deep love for the Word of God.

Steve is part artist and part engineer and he embraces the dynamic tension between the two. He has worked in aerospace, space and defense systems, semi-conductor, voice and data systems, and in the oil industry. And he loves to teach the Word.

Steve is an avid outdoorsman; surfing, fishing, snorkeling, kayaking, and collecting rocks. These loves have been greatly curtailed with the amputation of his left leg above the knee, but he celebrates the memories of those times and experiences.

He has known much pain and hardship and who amongst us hasn't. He writes what he has experienced. He writes from the heart.

Steve's book is addressed to Christian men who have struggled in their walk with the Lord, just as he has. He shares personal testimonies about his battles with the temptations known to all who love the Lord. And he shares of times the Lord has spoken specifically to him. His life is an open book.

Acknowledgements

First and foremost, I want to thank God for His leading me to write a book. It was something I have always wanted to do, but didn't know where to begin. I believe the Lord showed me.

I also offer my heartfelt thanks and deep appreciation to Pastor John Harp for his read of my book, and for the lengthy and deep comments he provided. His godly insight and his knowledge of the Word of God blessed me greatly. John holds a Master of Divinity Degree from Abilene Christian University and has been in full-time ministry for 38 years, all of which has been at the Sunset Ridge Church of Christ in San Antonio, Texas. He also ministers to the homeless and other people in need each Monday morning at Christian Assistance Ministry of San Antonio. Sunset Ridge Church's website is: www.sunsetridgechurch.org/

In spite of working a full time job, and supporting her husband in ministry, Kari Heitman was an invaluable and godly asset to me. Her excellent editorial and copy critiques, the challenging questions and comments she directed to me, and her syntax and grammar savvy were all so welcome and much needed. Her love for the Lord and for His Word was evident in all her support to me.

I want to acknowledge and thank artist, Todd Thomas, for diligently working with me to create the exceptional book cover art, and for his gracious patience with me throughout the process. His contact information is: Todd L. Thomas, Klamath Falls, Oregon 97601. Website is: www. ToddLThomas.com

---

I have many people to thank for their encouragement and prayers as I wrote. Number one amongst them is my beloved mother, Gail Rae Wilkinson. Her excitement about each chapter, her editorial inputs and comments, and her belief that such a book needed to be written, was such an encouragement to me, as is she. She loves the Lord, and His Word, more than anyone I have ever known or met.

Preface

There's a war going on. It's a spiritual battle and all too many Christian men have gone silent in the battle. Our heart is what is truly at issue here.

The berthing force behind this book is the phrase "to guard the hearts and minds of men." These words came to me many years ago in a unique and terrifying way. Allow me.

They came during a period in my life that I was struggling to provide for my wife and our firstborn daughter, Sarah. I had come to faith in Jesus Christ just a couple years earlier. I had a growing fire within me for Jesus Christ and for the Word of God. I sensed a call from God into ministry and others in my church recognized the same, yet I was locked into a job where I was physically, mentally, emotionally, financially, and spiritually drained.

For a number of years before going to college, I worked in an open air Quonset hut in an electrical motor shop in south Texas, just north of Galveston in support of the refiner's in the area. The work and work environment were filthy. There was no air conditioning in the summer and no heater in the winter. By noon, I was covered in electrical motor grease, the chemicals Varsol and Xylene, epoxy, ash from the burn out ovens, and sweat. At the time, I did not see God in that place, but I knew he was present within me.

I began to press God for an understanding of His will for my life and why I had so many day to day struggles, and the ongoing misery I was experiencing.

During that time period, there were nights while in bed that I would silently preach. The words just came to me, and I would continue to preach to who-knows-who until I had to get out of bed to change out of the T-shirt I had perspired through.

But there was one night where I did not preach. As my wife slept soundly beside me, I wrestled deeply with what the will of God was for me and about His call on my life. You know… why all the struggles? Why His silence?

That night while in bed and with eyes wide open, the bedroom suddenly illumined. A bright white and vivid static electricity audibly crackled and ran along the bedroom walls and corners. It lit the bedroom as it ran along and across the bed spread. The visible electricity even traced the outline of the bed cover I had pulled up to my nose in my attempt to hide myself, but from what? I was terrified!

As this continued, I wondered what in the world was happening. Then I became aware of words being audibly spoken, or I heard them as if audibly - I believe the former. I heard words being spoken even as I thought and spoke words to myself. It was as if there were two conversations happening in that room, both happening at the same time.

As I silenced myself, I heard two phrases spoken, each one more than once. The two phrases were 1) "be patient for now" and 2) "to guard the hearts and minds of men." As soon as whatever it was had happened, the room suddenly dimmed and I fell sound sleep.

The next day I wrote of it in my journal, lamenting that if I had only kept my mouth shut and thoughts silent, I might have heard everything spoken to me. ("Were they spoken to me?") I wanted context for what I heard and experienced the night before. I felt the fool for questioning what I saw and heard.

I had a sense about "be patient for now." I think the Lord asks that of me just about every day. But now I ask, "Lord, is this book I'm writing what those words were about that night - to guard the hearts and minds of men?"

I believe I am to share the challenges and struggles I have known in my life as a man, both since giving my heart and life to Jesus Christ and in the dark years of my life before coming to faith in Him. It was during those darks years that I began to fill my heart and mind with much of the content that I battle against to this day - that old nature within me. I know many of these same things are what Christian men and women struggle with today.

When I have been asked to speak or when I open a class I am teaching, typically co-ed classes, I'll state to those in attendance "You know, God made me a man, I will speak as a man." I am careful about what I share, but my life and my heart is an open book. I trust the leading of the Holy Spirit in what I have written and shared, and have asked that of Him in the writing of this book.

I have been blessed immensely in writing this. It has been, by far, the best prolonged in-depth Bible study I have ever experienced. I believe the Lord wanted that for me.

I have been led to include many Scriptures in this book - divinely inspired words of direction, correction, encouragement, and truth.

My prayer is that the reading of this book will be for our collective good and for the Glory of God. Ultimately, the only thing that truly matters is the Glory of God.

Let's begin…

Contents

Chapter 1

THE BATTLEGROUND

"For our struggle is not against flesh and blood, but against the rulers, against the powers, against the world forces of this darkness, against the spiritual forces of wickedness in the heavenly places." (Ephesians 6:12)

There is no battle when there is no opposing side.

We Are at War!

Men, there's a battle going on and this war was declared since the days of creation in the Garden of Eden and it rages today. Unlike the wars that world history records, this war is spiritual in nature. It surrounds us and confronts us from every side, wanting to engulf us.

There is not a single arena in the world that isn't involved in the struggle we face as Christian men. It's the battle for the hearts, minds, and souls of men who love and have embraced Jesus Christ as Savior and Lord, and it's the battle for men who have yet to give their lives to Him. My prayer is that this book will be the call to arms to each of us.

"He who dwells in the shelter of the Most High will rest in the shadow of the Almighty. I will say of the Lord, He is my refuge and my fortress, my God, in whom I trust. Surely he will save you from the fowler's snare and from the deadly pestilence. He will cover you with his feathers, and under his

1

> *wings you will find refuge; his faithfulness will be your shield
> and rampart" (Psalm 91:1-4)*

The very moment we come to faith in Jesus Christ we step into spiritual battle. It's unfortunate that this is rarely addressed with new believers. When new believers first experience attacks from the enemy, often they aren't aware that it is Satan behind the assault.

When a battle rages, those who take a neutral stance stand with the enemy.

Prior to coming to faith in Jesus Christ, we were Satan's children - and we frolicked and lived in his domain. But upon salvation we became Satan's enemy. We renounced him. Satan sees us as having betrayed him. The more we pursue Christ, the greater will be Satan's purpose to thwart us at every step. We appear on Satan's radar as a threat to his diabolical purposes.

> *"For all that is in the world, the lust of the flesh and the lust of
> the eyes and the boastful pride of life, is not from the Father,
> but is from the world. The world is passing away, and also
> its lusts; but the one who does the will of God lives forever."*
> *(1 John 2:16-17)*

The battlefronts in the war we are to be engaged in are many and varied. The three primary enemies of the Christian life are the world, the flesh, and the devil - the unholy trinity of this war. This unholy alliance is set against the hearts, minds, and souls of Christian men. We'll look briefly at each so as to set the table for what will follow.

The World

> *"Do not love the world nor the things in the world. If anyone
> loves the world, the love of the Father is not in him. (1 John
> 2:15)*

The world that assaults us is the value-laden system that controls and directs our society. It is diametrically opposed to the ways of God. By this definition, the world is a threat to us and to our spiritual well-being.

When Christians speak of the "world" we live in, we recognize that it is a man-centered construct of a selfish, me-centered, way of living. It is made up of ungodly principles and standards, and declares, "He who dies with the most toys wins!" To their eternal detriment, one who lives his or her life in this way gives spiritual values a distant second place in their lives.

The world represents all that is radically opposed to there being an almighty, all-powerful, all-knowing, and ever-present God. The world rejects God because to believe in God begs an answer to this question: "If there is a God, then how shall I so live?"

Those unbelievers around us, as if playing the man, are inviting us and challenging us, to participate in the subtle immorality of what gives life to them. We are assaulted by coarse words, sex-laced humor, and the like. They call it joking or just being funny, and even if we don't participate in the banter, still their words can so easily find residence in our minds. Those words, those jokes, and the thoughts they carry can come back to us at a later time.

> *"But immorality or any impurity or greed must not even be named among you, as is proper among saints; and there must be no filthiness and silly talk, or coarse jesting, which are not fitting, but rather giving of thanks. For this you know with certainty, that no immoral or impure person or covetous man, who is an idolater, has an inheritance in the kingdom of Christ and God."(Ephesians 5:3-5)*

Consider the far-reaching influence of television. Years ago television began to usurp the role of the church in American society, namely to shape our system of values and mores - our cultural norms. It's become a form of religion in and of itself. Key nationally televised "religious events" such as the Academy Awards and the Super Bowl lend to the television experience a sort of shared communion among the masses, as if a rite or ritual of great significance and meaning.

Television, rather than the church, became the place where many people found a worldview that reflects what is to them of ultimate value, justifying their behavior and way of life. People tend to feed on what the television serves up. But technology has exploded so far beyond the television in the past ten years or so. The mere issue of technology in this day is an entire matter unto itself.

The book of Daniel prophesied this regarding the ability to travel and the exponential growth of knowledge in our time:

> *But as for you, Daniel, conceal these words and seal up the book until the end of time; many will go back and forth, and knowledge will increase." (Daniel 12:4)*

Today, what the internet brings to a home is akin to a three-dimensional television experience in comparison to the more linear past. No longer is it a small handful of networks competing for an audience, but literally hundreds of options for us, sometimes hundreds of options within an option, as it is with Netflix and Amazon Prime.

> *"You adulteresses, do you not know that friendship with the world is hostility toward God? Therefore whoever wishes to be a friend of the world makes himself an enemy of God." (James 4:4)*

The James 4:4 passage is a strong and direct word to us. Friendship with the world puts us at odds with God. So much in this world competes for our undivided attention.

Social media promises happiness and satisfaction, but so-called friends are little more than a one-dimensional electronic presence somewhere in a cloud. No doubt you have seen, as I have, a family dining out together, seated at the same table, with each staring at their individual smart devices.

People sometimes even text someone they are seated next to. What has happened?

While driving home from work I would often lift my right hand and pray as I passed a so-called adult book store. I would pray for those who frequented this place. I prayed for conviction and for a sense of the Lord's presence.

One day while doing so, the thought came to me that a place just like this now exists in every home via our personal computers and through the smart devices we own. The thought chilled me, but it is so true. There is no end to what competes for our attention - often our undivided attention.

The world's roads are littered with billboards full of words and pictures that play to the hearts and imaginations of men. Images appear on our computers and our smart phones, calling out to us and enticing us to do just a little further investigation. The lyrics in the songs we listen to have a similar effect in that they play to that something desired or something missing in our lives. They scream to give us license to pursue that which they call us to.

Commercials we watch target our wants and the fear of missing out - FOMO. We are being told to want this, buy that, look like this, and behave like this.

The world wants to draw us deeper into its clutches and further away from our Savior. The politically-correct drum beat that sounds daily wants to mute our call to be salt and light in this world.

Regarding Our Sexual Identity...

> *"So God created man in his own image, in the image of God he created him; male and female he created them." (Genesis 1:27)*

Why the confusion in the world today about our sexual identity? When I was younger you were either a boy or a girl, and that made sense to me.

It seemed as simple as this: you either had one or you didn't. You know what I mean? Yet in today's downward spiral of all things God-centered, the world via social media now offers us sixty something ways by which to define ourselves - our sexual selves.

We must be on guard not only for our sexual identity in Christ, but also of the sexual purity of our wives and children and their sexual identity. The meaning of the words that worldly people use has changed dramatically in the days we live in. Our language has morphed.

In *1984*, George Orwell wrote, "Change the language [the words we use] and you change the logic."

This book is not about our sexual identity. It is about the war we Christian men are in and sexual identity is one of the arenas where this battle is being played out against us. Maleness and manhood are under full attack today. We see it being played out daily around us.

The world wants to emasculate men and masculinize women.

While in college (and a very liberal college at that) I once spoke before those in the Speech class I was enrolled in about the imminent return of Jesus Christ. I pulled no punches. I spoke about some of the signs of His soon return, speaking about the growing number of earthquakes that will come like a woman in birth pangs, growing in frequency and intensity as the day approaches. Reality continues to note this – earthquakes everywhere - yet we hear very little of it on the news, as if to deny the truth of it.

When I finished my speech, the room was dead silent. After I seated myself the class professor, sitting on his desk, looked at the class and asked, "Well, what do you think?" The pregnant pause that followed his question was telling.

My brother, we must speak as if we, too, have the courage of Joshua (reference the book of Joshua, chapters 1-3).

> *"Only be strong and very courageous; be careful to do according to all the law which Moses My servant commanded you; do not turn from it to the right or to the left, so that you may have success wherever you go." (Joshua 1:7 and numerous places elsewhere in the book of Joshua)*

Don't let the unbelieving world silence us. To my point, and much to my surprise, a young man in that Speech class approached me after the class and pulled me into an empty room. He wanted to know more. Frankly, he was about the last person in that class that I could ever imagine coming to Christ, but he became a believer that day.

You never know who is listening.

We must overcome the world by separating ourselves from it. Not that we might become some sort of other-worldly vagabond or religious isolationist, but rather that we refuse to be guided by the world's standards of right and wrong.

> **One day God will remove His church from the world, but today He's removing the world from His church.**

The Flesh

> *"Now the deeds of the flesh are evident, which are: immorality, impurity, sensuality, idolatry, sorcery, enmities, strife, jealousy, outbursts of anger, disputes, dissensions, factions, envying, drunkenness, carousing, and things like these, of which I forewarn you, just as I have forewarned you, that those who practice such things will not inherit the kingdom of God. (Galatians 5:19-21)*

In regards to our battle against the flesh, biblestudytools.com, in an article called "Spiritual Warfare: Understanding the Battle," notes the following:

"For some of us, the hardest battles are fought within ourselves. We can understand the circumstances and situations that the enemy uses to destroy

us. We can accept the truth of how the world lures and tempts us. We can understand to some degree that the battle in the spiritual realm is ongoing and real, even though we cannot see it. But to get a grasp on what is going on within our own hearts and minds can be the hardest, most exhausting, battle of them all."

Those are true words. Our eyes are the open portal through which the images we see or entertain find residence in our hearts and minds. The old fleshly nature within us lusts for things we do not have, or we lust for more and more of it. Suggestively clad women compete for our attention and affections. What man can't help but recognize the initial attractiveness of a beautiful or physically appealing woman, but we own the second look.

> *"You have heard that it was said, 'YOU SHALL NOT COMMIT ADULTERY'; but I say to you that everyone who looks at a woman with lust for her has already committed adultery with her in his heart. If your right eye makes you stumble, tear it out and throw it from you; for it is better for you to lose one of the parts of your body, than for your whole body to be thrown into hell. (Matthew 5:27-29)*

The assault upon us is against Christian men of all ages.

Regarding Lust...

> *"For all that is in the world, the lust of the flesh and the lust of the eyes and the boastful pride of life, is not from the Father, but is from the world." (1 John 2:16)*

Lust is an uncontrollable desire for a given object of interest. Lust for anything can easily be defined as that drug of choice that calls out to us when our circumstances seem overwhelming or when we feel great disappointment or hurt. I will employ the use of the phrase, "our drug of choice," in various places throughout this book.

To lust for something doesn't only apply to the desire for physical or sexual pleasure. We can lust for any number of things. Money, power, prestige, position, fishing – you name it.

Lust can be defined as follows:

1. not within proper or reasonable limits; out of bounds; excessive

2. unrestrained in conduct, feelings: an inordinate admirer of beauty

3. disorderly; uncontrolled

4. not regulated; irregular

5. An overwhelming desire or craving.

Lust is an inordinate love of anything that replaces Jesus Christ as central in our lives.

The flesh, our old nature, screams to be catered to. Our flesh wants to be God. Before coming to faith in Jesus Christ we went about filling ourselves with things that we, at the time, thought would bring us pleasure, or comfort, or bring ease to that something is missing sense within us. We went about stuffing into that God-shaped vacuum what we felt was missing in our lives at the time. Those very things remain there, in our heart, and await our beckon call. That something missing was God and only He can fill that vacuum.

Our flesh wants to be God.

Regarding Temptation...

> *"No temptation has overtaken you except what is common to mankind. And God is faithful; he will not let you be tempted beyond what you can bear. But when you are tempted, he will also provide a way out so that you can endure it." (1 Corinthians 10:13)*

I believe one of the most effective weapons that the world, the flesh, and the devil employs is temptation. In what has been referred to as the genealogy of death, James 1:13-15a says of temptation, this:

> *"Let no one say when he is tempted, "I am being tempted by God"; for God cannot be tempted by evil, and He Himself does not tempt anyone. But each one is tempted when he is carried away and enticed by his own lust. Then when lust has conceived, it gives birth to sin; and when sin is accomplished, it brings forth death." (James 1:13-15a)*

Yes, God does test His children, but He never tempts us to do evil and sin. It is often mankind's tendency, our natural inclination, to blame God for our own mistakes, our times of misbehavior, and for the failures, the disappointments, and the filth in our lives. We rationalize these things and we tend to prescribe rational lies about them. Men, we've got to own our sin – that very stuff that already exists in our heart.

The point here is obvious - When we're tempted we cannot blame God for it. Temptation is not found in any external circumstance, person or object, but rather comes from our own sinful desires that reside within us.

There are precautions we can exercise when facing temptation. First and foremost – simply avoid sinful behavior. I know that sounds rather obvious, but it must be stated.

> *"But keep on the alert at all times, praying that you may have strength to escape all these things that are about to take place and to stand before the Son of Man." (Luke 21:36)*

Again, be on the alert. There are certain places and locations that have the potential to spark ungodly thoughts and influence over us and from within us; so don't go there! We are to know our weaknesses and our limitations. Why run to the very thing that would destroy you? Keep your eyes and your focus straight ahead. See Jesus.

Satan uses the many enticements of the world and the appeal of the flesh to try and get us to do what God forbids - to take our primary focus off of Jesus Christ. He wants to allure us back into the realm we were freed from when we gave our hearts and lives to Jesus Christ.

Take heart, my brother. We can overcome the flesh by denying it and to just say no to the desires of our fallen nature that reside within us. But to just say no is NOT enough. None of us possess the strength and power to do this victoriously.

Before we were saved, we lived in darkness - let's call it the cave. I remember the cave that Jesus Christ drew me out of. It's the very cave I have sometimes found myself shamefully revisiting from time to time in my walk with Him. While we were in that cave, we were in total darkness, unexposed to the light. We were not even aware that light existed - it was more a feel than see environment.

But through the miracle of the new birth, we became a new creature in Christ. However, those old tapes that once played within our minds remain. By studying and memorizing God's Word, you can break old sinful thought patterns and actions. We can be set free from dark, debilitating thoughts. As we ask God to remove the old, the Holy Spirit brings new thoughts to our minds. Old urges disappear under His protective care. We'll look more deeply at this later.

We can avoid temptation by asking God to reprogram our thinking. We will examine this, the renewing of our minds, in chapter 3.

The Devil

> *"Your enemy the devil prowls around like a roaring lion looking for someone to devour. Resist him, standing firm in the faith." (1 Peter 5:8-9)*

Satan hates none of God's creation more than he does Christians.

Satan is the supreme commander of this unholy trinity we war against - the world, the flesh, and the devil. Satan's schemes are powerful and persuasive. He is the master of his art – which is the art of deception. He is a liar! I have heard it said that when he lies, he speaks his native language.

Satan wants to devour us - to emasculate and neuter us. Satan wants to silence Christian men so that we're unable to reproduce our own kind – other Christians. And he can silence us in any number of ways.

- He wants to rob us of our testimony by tempting us to sin and, in doing so, he silences us.
- He wants to pollute our faith by bringing doubt - doubt about the goodness of God and doubt of His Word.
- He wants to assault our acts of worship - to silence us in our proclamation of the holiness and glory of our God. *(Satan hates our worship!)*
- He wants to interrupt our good deeds and to silence our acts of charity and our acts of service to others.
- He wants to isolate us and draw us away from the flock. Before coming to Jesus Christ, we were the Lone Ranger of our own lives, and we can so easily be drawn back to that way of thinking, that way of living. Again, Satan wants to silence us.

Likely you have known someone who has said to you, "I believe." When I hear someone say that, I must ask, "What is it you believe?"

People believe all kinds of things, but belief alone does not bring someone to salvation. There must be conviction about the state we find ourselves in. There must be a bowing of the head and heart in repentance and there must be an acknowledgement of and a full surrender to the lordship of our risen Savior, Jesus Christ.

Satan believes everything about Jesus and he hates what he believes.

If Satan is left unopposed, he'll do what he can to redirect us, to entice us back to the dark places we once willfully inhabited - back to those sexual desires and images that are chemically etched into our minds. He wants us to draw upon them like the drinking of putrid water.

Those private reserves that we warehouse in our hearts are actually the presence and domain of Satan within us. This is why we must take every thought captive to our Lord and Savior Jesus Christ. 2 Corinthians 10:3-5 states this clearly:

> *"For though we walk in the flesh, we do not war according to the flesh, for the weapons of our warfare are not of the flesh, but divinely powerful for the destruction of fortresses. We are destroying speculations and every lofty thing raised up against the knowledge of God, and we are taking every thought captive to the obedience of Christ," (2 Corinthians 10:3-5)*

In the physical warfare that is typical in this world, we can visualize and see the enemy. We know of his presence by reconnaissance - our military observation of a region to locate an enemy or ascertain strategic features. We gather intel about his whereabouts, plot it on a map, and in doing so we can ascertain how best to strike out at him and what weapons to employ so as to defeat him – at least in a given arena or theater of operation.

In the great spiritual conflict we are in DAILY, we cannot physically see Satan's whereabouts. If we could we would be rocked by his immediacy because the enemy of our soul is ever around us. The intel we can gather about our enemy, his presence, his schemes and strategies, comes first to us from the Word of God.

The fortresses we battle for are those fortresses that exist in our own hearts - the very ground we have surrendered to the enemy. We must reclaim that territory. We must refill our hearts with God's Word so that in times of challenge, fear, temptation, etc., we can respond out of the new nature the Lord has given us.

> *"Therefore if anyone is in Christ, he is a new creature; the old things passed away; behold, new things have come." (2 Corinthians 5:17)*

There are areas in our hearts that the enemy claims hold to. The territory we are to regain in this lifelong conflict with Satan is the territory within us that needs to be leveled. This can only happen with the continual infilling of both the Word of God and of the Holy Spirit of God into our hearts, minds, and lives.

Satan wants to defeat us. He wants to defeat us and all those who have embraced salvation through Jesus Christ. He wants to silence our testimony and he'll toss every lure at his disposal at us to do so.

We can overcome the devil by resisting him. We must take a determined stand against Satan and not give him a foothold, or a renewed one, that he once held in our lives. We must not take the bait.

Yes, we are in a war, but we are not alone in this battle. We have fellow believers, brothers and sisters in Christ that stand with us. In his book, *Wild at Heart*, John Eldredge states:

> **We don't need accountability groups, we need fellow warriors, someone to fight alongside us, someone to watch our back.**

> *"Blessed be the Lord, my rock, who trains my hands for war, and my fingers for battle;" (Psalms 144:1)*

Visualizing the Battle

I have always liked sculptures, especially Westerns in bronze or pewter. I own a sculpture of a cowboy attempting to stay in the saddle on a wildly bucking bronco. It is by a sculptor named Buck McCain and is titled 'Clash of the Wills' (The Franklin Mint, 1981). When I see that pewter sculpture I see myself as being that cowboy (that Christian cowboy) on that wild horse (my old nature). I see a stark visual image of my old nature desperately trying to throw me. That old nature I battle with daily that I inherited from Adam, but as a child of the King, I own the call to stay on the saddle – in Christ.

There's a Scripture that comes to my spirit about the battle I am in daily to overcome my old nature. It's Philippians 2:12-13:

> *"So then, my beloved, just as you have always obeyed, not as in my presence only, but now much more in my absence, work out your salvation with fear and trembling; for it is God who is at work in you, both to will and to work for His good pleasure." (Philippians 2:12-13)*

Again, when it comes to temptation or lust or any other specific area of challenge, the struggle we are in does not come from an external source, it comes from what already exists in our own hearts. That's the old nature we all battle with.

> *"Suffer hardship with me, as a good soldier of Christ Jesus. No soldier in active service entangles himself in the affairs of everyday life, so that he may please the one who enlisted him as a soldier." (2 Timothy 2:3-4)*

That Which Calls Out to Us

Proverbs 7 speaks of the battleground we walk amidst daily in our walk with Christ. It speaks of the stuff within us that still calls out to us. We are to remain in the saddle, in Christ, as the world, the flesh (our old nature), and the devil fights to throw us off.

Proverbs 7:6-23 offers an excellent teaching about that which calls out to us. But I want to begin with the direct words of instruction to us in Proverbs 7:1-5.

> *"My son, keep my words and treasure my commandments within you. Keep my commandments and live, and my teaching as the apple of your eye. Bind them on your fingers; write them on the tablet of your heart. Say to wisdom, "You are my sister," And call understanding your intimate friend; that they may keep you from an adulteress, from the foreigner who flatters with her words." (Proverbs 7:1-5)*

These first five verses of Proverbs 7 are the instructions we are given because there are things in our lives like thoughts, feelings, emotions, and lust-driven inclinations that call out to us and that our old nature clings to. The following Proverbs 7 verses unpack the truth of this.

Proverbs 7:6-9 (into the darkness)

> *"For at the window of my house I looked out through my lattice, and I saw among the naive, and discerned among the youths a young man lacking sense, passing through the street near her corner; and he takes the way to her house, in the twilight, in the evening, in the middle of the night and in the darkness." (Proverbs 7:6-9)*

Near her corner: See that this young man lacking sense doesn't initially make a direct bee-line to the thing that calls out to him, but he soon finds himself in her neighborhood. And the closer he gets to her, the stronger the pull is.

***Regardless of the time of day, it is always into
spiritual darkness that this thing calls us into.***

Proverbs 7:10-20 (the attraction of what calls out to us)

> *"And behold, a woman comes to meet him, dressed as a harlot
> and cunning of heart. She is boisterous and rebellious, her
> feet do not remain at home; She is now in the streets, now
> in the squares, and lurks by every corner. So she seizes him
> and kisses him and with a brazen face she says to him: "I
> was due to offer peace offerings; today I have paid my vows.
> "Therefore I have come out to meet you, to seek your presence
> earnestly, and I have found you. "I have spread my couch
> with coverings, with colored linens of Egypt. "I have sprinkled
> my bed with myrrh, aloes and cinnamon. "Come, let us drink
> our fill of love until morning; let us delight ourselves with
> caresses. "For my husband is not at home, he has gone on a
> long journey; He has taken a bag of money with him, at the
> full moon he will come home." (Proverbs 7:10-20)*

Whatever it is that calls out to us justifies our interests in it. The allurement
speaks to our hearts and minds as if to say "go ahead - no one will know"
(verses 19-20). But God knows.

She is now in the streets… and lurks by every corner: In the fallen world we
live in, the "she" that attracts us is EVERYWHERE. Once we have come
face to face with what it is that has called out to us, everything suddenly
justifies itself, as do her cunning words to the naïve young man.

Proverbs 7:21-23 (led to slaughter)

> *"With her many persuasions she entices him; with her
> flattering lips she seduces him. Suddenly he follows her as an
> ox goes to the slaughter, or as one in fetters to the discipline
> of a fool, Until an arrow pierces through his liver; as a bird
> hastens to the snare, so he does not know that it will cost him
> his life" (Proverbs 7:21-23)*

I have heard such words spoken; I've been this ox.

When an ox is led somewhere, it has no idea where it's being led. Our drug of choice will lead us to slaughter and once under its full pull, we rarely resist, and often we are unable even to do so. Then the inevitable happens. We do indeed reap what we sow; see Galatians 6:7.

———————————————

Proverbs 7:21-23 brings to mind a fishing illustration. All my life I have loved to fish, so now after growing up on the east coast of southern Florida, living on the West Coast, and after many years of fishing the Gulf Coast, I am especially fond of saltwater fishing. Whether fishing is an interest or passion to you, this story will speak to you of the temptations that are tossed our way.

The Lure of Temptation

I wonderfully recall as an elementary aged boy the near rapture of hooking into a fish that I could not fight nor turn. I remember older men laughing at me hollering, "Boy, you better cut the line!"

What I am about to share I heard from an older Godly Christian man who also liked to fish. He made quick mention of this to me just after I got saved. Over the years I have added a lot to the thought because of the challenges I was experiencing in my early walk with Jesus. It's about being enticed and plays out like this:

See in your mind's eye a large, fat, and sassy largemouth bass as he is taking rest under the submerged logs he considers home. Let's call him Mr. Bass.

Having eaten earlier that morning, Mr. Bass is not really hungry and has no interest to feed at the time. But from somewhere just out of his sight a shiny lure is cast and hits the water's surface. He hears it. After dropping several inches below the surface, that lure begins to move forward in a practiced rhythmic manner as it nears Mr. Bass's abode.

Mr. Bass sees it. He takes note how it shines and the calculated fluctuations of its movements tempts his further interest. Now, taking a second look, he watches it more intently. As the lure nears him, suddenly, almost instinctively, Mr. Bass shoots out from his protective cover and strikes it full force!

For a brief moment Mr. Bass is excited. He has full hold upon it, but he soon realizes that something is amiss. This is no meal. It feels and tastes unlike what he had expected. Try as he did, he couldn't dislodge it from his mouth. It was then he knew he should have never taken that second look at it.

Several thoughts about the late Mr. Bass (and about you and me):

1. Mr. Bass wasn't hungry at the time - he was simply at home minding his own business.
2. A temptation was tossed his way. He did not see who threw the lure. Frankly, he didn't even know it was a lure. But whatever it was, it called out to him and he entertained the thought.
3. Now fully-enticed, Mr. Bass was drawn out from his protective covering so as to pursue his interest. Not only did he pursue it, he took full grip upon it.
4. Suddenly, rather than his having it, it had him. It wasn't until after he had what he thought he so desired, it cost him his life.

Several thoughts about the lure:

1. Obviously, the lure (that which calls out to us) was cast by the devil, the unseen fisherman in the story.
2. The devil knew where Mr. Bass lived and, by having observed Mr. Bass's tendencies, he knew what would entice him.
3. The enemy is very practiced at making the lure very appealing. He knows how to entice us and Satan always promises more than he can deliver.
4. When we take hold of that which the enemy lures us out to, we, in essence, surrender ourselves to the enemy. Not only did he

discontinue producing any more baby bass, Mr. Bass took the bait and died that day - hook, line, and sinker.

"I have made a covenant with my eyes; how then could I gaze at a virgin? And what is the portion of God from above or the heritage of the Almighty from on high? Is it not calamity to the unjust and disaster to those who work iniquity?" (Job 31:1-3)

Men, as I've stated before, we are to be careful with our eyes; we cannot help but initially recognize the beauty or attraction of a given woman or some other temptation or allurement, but we must own that second thought of it or look at it.

With her flattering lips she seduces him. Yes she does. Mr. Bass was seduced. My point is that it does not have to be a woman that calls out to us. Whatever it is that calls out to us, we can so easily become enticed into desiring it, or to desire it again. And once we have embraced it, we in effect cling to the very thing that will destroy us.

I once shared Proverbs 7 and the Mr. Bass story with some men who were prison inmates. Everyone one of them saw the truth of it. Everyone one of them agreed that the something that called out to them was the very thing that led them to prison, or back to prison.

Proverbs 7:24-27 – do not stray…

"Now therefore, my sons, listen to me, and pay attention to the words of my mouth. Do not let your heart turn aside to her ways, do not stray into her paths. For many are the victims she has cast down, and numerous are all her slain. Her house is the way to Sheol, descending to the chambers of death." (Proverbs 7:24-27)

The inspired Word of God instructs us on how to address our struggle with that which calls out to us in the next chapter of Proverbs, Proverbs 8. I encourage you to read it for yourself.

Men, we must remain on guard about yielding to our drug of choice for the pain, fear, or disappointment we are feeling. My brothers, we must count the cost! The true battleground in the war we are in is the battle for our hearts. The truth of this cannot be understated. Our understanding of this war must begin with matters of the heart. In God's economy, it's always about the heart.

Never forget - Satan perverts the truth. He desires to redirect us – he'll tempt us again and again. He attempted to do so with Jesus while in the wilderness for forty days. As with Jesus, Satan even uses Scripture to do so, but always with a twist, a perversion of the truth of the Word of God. We must remain on guard to Satan's methods and schemes. I've seen him at work in this very thing.

The first casualty of any war is truth.

Early in my walk with Jesus Christ I had a great burden about the New Age movement.

Regarding the New Age Movement, in Neil Anderson's book, *Walking Through the Darkness,* he writes: "The New Age movement is not seen as a religion but a new way to think and understand reality. It's very attractive to the natural man who has become disillusioned with organized religion and Western rationalism. He desires spiritual reality but doesn't want to give up materialism, deal with his moral problems, or come under authority"

In the late eighties I heard about a New Age get together that was to be held at a city park near us and decided I was going! I encouraged my mom (who loves Jesus more than any other person I have ever known) and my then wife to attend with me. As we neared the park, I noticed a large, tall wooden cross mounted upright in the bed of a pick-up truck parked at a nearby grocery store, so I pulled up to investigate. I called the brother near it over and expressed my joy at seeing his witness. "Yeah, man, there's a big New Age thing goin' on across the street, so we're prayin' for them!"

"Awesome" I exclaimed. "And while you're praying, pray for us – we're going!"

I could recount pages of information about what we saw and experienced there. Me, I was all eyes and heart. Under a large pavilion I saw a display of beautiful quartz crystals, likely from the mines in Arkansas. Being an avid rock hound I had to speak to the young man behind the table about them. We spoke briefly about the minerals he had on display. I knew they were more than just rocks to him, so I asked "Other than a source of revenue, what do you see in these quartz crystals?"

His eyes sort of rolled back into his head at the question. Then he leaned forward towards me and semi-whispered, "Why, just last night I contacted three extraterrestrials through them!"

I told him I didn't doubt for a minute that he had made some sort of contact, but I assured him they were not extraterrestrials that he experienced.

Shortly after the crystal conversation, the main attraction of this event took place. Apparently some well-known female channeler was to speak. It was surreal to see the mass of people flock to her - pun intended.

They were invited to sit on the ground in a large semi-circle around her - some fifty or more folks did so. My mom and wife were a little nervous and kind of watched from a distance. I stood to the immediate right of this channeler. Only her two male body guards were closer to her than I was.

Before she began to speak, three men came into the center of the large semi-circle and then laid flat on their backs on the ground. Each man then had a very large clear glass bowl placed on each of their stomachs. As they laid there three other people each began to rub their hands around the rims of the bowls.

The sounds emitted from those huge glass bowls were an eerie wailing drone that would sort of rise and fall in tone and volume. It was a call to their spirit guides to come to join them. After several minutes they halted. (That sound was the only thing that really creeped me out that day.)

Then she began to speak.

I wish I had notes or a recording of what I heard. As she spoke, she'd reference the Bible, but she continually misquoted or twisted what the Word says; she spoke woefully out of context. I do not recall how long she spoke.

After she finished speaking, one of her male bodyguards took her microphone and offered to all present to come forward so she could 'read their aura' (or something like that). This call to those present was as if a sickening altar call, and why not. Satan is the ultimate rip-off artist. He loves religion. I was the first to approach her.

I began by lovingly pointing out to her that she had misquoted Scripture. I offered a couple examples of her doing so using her own words. Then I quoted the Scripture and offered context to it. I did so for only a minute or two.

At that point, her two bodyguards got closer to me so as to silence me. She approached me, raised her eyebrows and then spoke to me like some sort of robot saying, "I see in you a great deal of fear and anxiety."

I smiled replying, "God has not given me a spirit of fear, but of power and love and a sound mind. You need to take another look."

> *"For God hath not given us the spirit of fear; but of power, and of love, and of a sound mind. (2 Timothy 1:7, KJV)*

As she looked at me, her eyes got real big, reminding me of a 5th grade teacher I once had, but she was silent – as if she had been silenced.

Yes, people will believe just about anything.

At the Heart of the Battle

My brothers, we are called into battle. It's a battle for truth, God's truth, and it is a battle for the hearts, minds, and souls of the men and women who love Him. It's a battle for those that do not yet know the Lord. We must proclaim His goodness and wondrous truths. We are to be as a watchman on the wall; ever vigilant. Our nation slumbers.

> *"So then let us not sleep as others do, but let us be alert and self-controlled." (1 Thessalonians 5:6)*

Jeremiah 6:17-19 speaks to the deafness of our nation in this day:

> *"And I set watchmen over you, saying, 'Listen to the sound of the trumpet!' But they said, 'We will not listen.' "Therefore hear, O nations, and know, O congregation, what is among them. "Hear, O earth: behold, I am bringing disaster on this people, the fruit of their plans, because they have not listened to My words, and as for My law, they have rejected it also. (Jeremiah 6:17-19)*

We are, indeed in a battle. Today much of the church at large in America is asleep at the wheel. Are we? Are you?

> ### *The sleeper must awaken.*

> *"This is what the Lord says to you: 'Do not be afraid or discouraged because of this vast army. For the battle is not yours, but God's." (2 Chronicles 20:15)*

Study Guide - Chapter 1

Day 1

a) What battles are you presently fighting, both physically and spiritually? Open yourself up to this question.
b) What have you seen or experienced in the battles you have known?

c) From what front in your life have you known either an attack or resistance from Satan?

d) Where have you seen the enemy's hand in your life? Allow the below passage to speak of these things to you.

Passage: *"For our struggle is not against flesh and blood, but against the rulers, against the powers, against the world forces of this darkness, against the spiritual forces of wickedness in the heavenly places." (Ephesians 6:12)*

Response:

Day 2

a) What encouragement do you receive from the Luke 10:19 passage below? How do you define 'authority' as is given below?

Passage: *"Behold, I have given you authority to tread on serpents and scorpions, and over all the power of the enemy, and nothing shall hurt you." (Luke 10:19)*

Response:

b) Read the passage below and restate it in your own words.

c) Consider the phrase "you adulteresses" and make note of areas in your walk with Jesus Christ where you have acted as such.

Passage: *You adulteresses, do you not know that friendship with the world is hostility toward God? Therefore whoever wishes to be a friend of the world makes himself an enemy of God. (James 4:4)*

Response:

Day 3

a) What assault on your masculinity have you experienced, if any?
b) Who or where has it come from? Be honest with yourself about this; likely there is a level of hurt associated with what you have experienced.
c) In the battle with your old nature, what areas of interest or concern have proven the most difficult to wage war against?
d) What have been some of the difficulties you have faced?

Response:

Day 4

a) What sometimes calls out to you?
b) When is it that you might expect it to do so? Analyze those times so as to better understand why the things that call out to you do so.
c) How does the statement "The Sleeper Must Awaken" speak to you?
d) Where have you found yourself "in slumber" in your walk with Jesus Christ?

Response:

Day 5

Read and briefly comment on each of the following scriptural passages. Make note of the encouragement and strength you find in them - personalize them.

Passage: *"But the Lord is faithful, and he will strengthen you and protect you from the evil one." (2 Thessalonians 3:3)*

Response:

Passage: *"The thief comes only to steal and kill and destroy. I came that they may have life and have it abundantly." (John 10:10)*

Response:

Passage: *"the one who practices sin is of the devil; for the devil has sinned from the beginning. The Son of God appeared for this purpose, to destroy the works of the devil." (1 John 3:8)*

Response:

Passage: *"Submit yourselves to God. Resist the devil, and he will flee from you." (James 4:7)*

Response:

Passage: *"No temptation has seized you except what is common to man. And God is faithful; he will not let you be tempted beyond what you can bear. But when you are tempted, he will also provide a way out so that you can stand up under it." (1 Corinthians 10:13; NIV)*

Response:

Passage: *Search me, O God, and know my heart; Try me and know my anxious thoughts; and see if there be any hurtful way in me, And lead me in the everlasting way. (Psalm 139:23-24)*

Response:

Chapter 2
THE HEART OF MAN

"The heart is more deceitful than all else and is desperately sick; who can understand it?" (Jeremiah 17:9)

The Heart of the Matter

While investigating the Scriptures for a solid lead-in passage about the heart of man, I chose these three, including the Jeremiah passage above.

> *"And He was saying, "That which proceeds out of the man, that is what defiles the man. For from within, out of the heart of men, proceed the evil thoughts, fornications, thefts, murders, adulteries, deeds of coveting and wickedness, as well as deceit, sensuality, envy, slander, pride and foolishness. All these evil things proceed from within and defile the man." (Mark 7:20-23)*

> *"Above all else, guard your heart, for everything you do flows from it." (Psalm 4:23)*

The first passage, Jeremiah 17:9, is a truth we must embrace about ourselves. We were all born in sin. Thus, prior to coming to faith in Christ, we filled our hearts with anything and everything, whether willfully or by default. We then proceeded to add to and build upon the corruption that we housed within ourselves.

The second passage, Mark 7:20-23, is a laundry list of the contents of that corrupt database - that old nature within us. These are the very words Jesus spoke to His disciples and to us dealing with defilement.

The third passage, Proverbs 4:23, points clearly to the fact that everything we think or do flows out from our heart. We draw from all that exists within our heart and we put it into action by our thoughts, words, and deeds.

We'll look more deeply into these truths as we now begin a look at the heart of man. Consider this chapter a heart exam.

What God's Word says about the Heart of Man

What we warehouse and store in our hearts, the mind dwells on. We will look at the stuff within us and how it got there. But before we look at the battleground for the heart of man, let's examine what the Word of God says about our hearts.

> *"But the things that proceed out of the mouth come from the heart, and those defile the man. For out of the heart come evil thoughts, murders, adulteries, fornications, thefts, false witness, slanders. These are the things which defile the man;"* *(Matthew 15:18-20a)*

The passage above is much a restatement of Mark 7:20-23. The thought came to me that most men aren't naturally inclined to think we have a heart, as if that is too touchy a consideration or something. I mean really, when was the last time a man purposefully told you something about his inner self – about something deep from within his heart? Physically, we're fully aware of it, but the heart I speak of is much deeper and it's central to who we are as men. Jeremiah is straight to the point on what our heart is.

> *"The heart is more deceitful than all else and is desperately sick; who can understand it? I, the Lord, search the heart; I test the mind, even to give to each man according to his ways, according to the results of his deeds." (Jeremiah 17:9-10)*

I do not consider the passage above as bad news - it's the TRUTH. To fully understand and appreciate the great battle we are in, we must first embrace what the Word of God says about us. The Jeremiah passage should all but knock the air out of any of us if we think - even if but for a moment – "I'm good."

The Word says our heart is very deceitful because of our fallen nature before coming to faith in Jesus Christ. It is chocked full of everything that we have placed in it throughout the years of our lives. It is the reservoir, or database, from which we draw upon to make sense of our lives, and it is corrupt.

Our heart is the seat of our emotions, self-worth, trust, and desires. Too often we fall into the devil's traps because we make our decisions based on how we feel, or what we want at the moment, rather than on what is right and true.

When the passage states that *"I, God, search the heart," (verse 7:10),* He does so to reveal to us what is within it. God says, *"I test the mind,"* because the heart and mind go hand in hand. The mind dwells on what already exists in the heart. Again, our thoughts, words, and deeds are a result of what exists in the heart and the mind of each of us.

LORD, search my heart and test me. Show me any wicked way in me.

How many times have you blown it in any number of ways, especially verbally, only to ask yourself, "where did that come from?" Brothers, it came from within our own hearts.

The Word of God says our hearts are deceitful and desperately sick. Surely this isn't to say that every thought or action need be of itself something that is desperately sick, but rather that we, by nature, tend to draw upon bad data from our old nature to make sense of a thing. That's why we need spiritual renewal daily in our lives.

One of the easiest ways to understand what we have filled our hearts with is to inventory all the things that we have taken into ourselves in an attempt to fill the God-shaped vacuum in our hearts. He wants to be our number one - God must be number one.

> *"How can I know all the sins lurking in my heart? Cleanse me from these hidden faults. Keep your servant from deliberate sins! Don't let them control me. Then I will be free of guilt and innocent of great sin. May the words of my mouth and the meditation of my heart be pleasing to you, O Lord, my rock and my redeemer." (Psalms 19:12-14)*

The Psalmist acknowledges that there is stuff in our heart that we are not fully aware of, and much of it is hidden. Remember, it is human nature to keep under lock and key the myriad of hurts and pains we have suffered in our lives. Right alongside those things is the database of the drugs of choice that we often call upon to manage or suppress those painful memories and feelings.

Our heart is the private storehouse where we stash what we have taken into ourselves over the years, either visually, emotionally, or experientially and we tend to lock and guard this storehouse. It's like a garage where no vehicle is parked. Over time it becomes stuffed with you-name-it.

Finally, one day we break down and undertake the work to clean out our garage. Things you haven't seen or have forgotten about suddenly appear. You likely wonder, "Where did this come from?" as you open and sort out the myriad of items you uncover and more often than not, it is stuff you have no need of or interest in.

I've heard it said that our identify isn't found in what we own, but in who owes us. Matthew 6:19-21 speaks of this:

> *Do not store up for yourselves treasures on earth, where moth and rust destroy, and where thieves break in and steal. But store up for yourselves treasures in heaven, where neither moth nor rust destroys, and where thieves do not break in or steal; for where your treasure is, there your heart will be also. (Matthew 6:19-21)*

Our hearts must be renewed and renewal can come only by filling our heart with the Word of God - the needed spiritual data we can draw upon when we are under attack just as Jesus Christ did while being tempted in the wilderness (Luke 4:1-13). We must be about filling our heart with God's Word so that it trumps what is within us.

> *"We demolish arguments and every pretension that sets itself up against the knowledge of God, and we take captive every thought to make it obedient to Christ." (2 Corinthians 10:5)*

Again, not every thought is wrong or disobedient, but the Word of God says we must take every thought captive to Christ. Thoughts, especially tempting ones, either already have a stronghold in our heart, or they will try to make room for themselves there. Cancer begins as a single cell.

I often find myself under attack early in the morning. Sometimes, as I re-close my eyes so as to capture a little more slumber, a sexually lustful thought comes to mind. At that very instant, I must take that thought captive to Christ. If I don't, the thought continues and I, in my still sleepy weariness, am prone to consider the thought and to nurture it to my liking. Hebrews 12:1 (New Living Translation) speaks this so personally to me in saying:

> *Therefore, since we are surrounded by such a huge crowd of witnesses to the life of faith, let us strip off every weight that slows us down, **especially the sin that so easily trips us up.** And let us run with endurance the race God has set before us. (Hebrews 12:1, emphasis mine; NLT)*

Our hearts, when under examination by the indwelling Holy Spirit of God, does inventory on everything that is within us, but we must invite Him to do so.

I experienced a heart examination years ago during communion. As I lifted the communion cup to my lips and drew it to my mouth, that plastic cup became a mirror. That cup reflected to me the struggles and stumbles I had experienced that very week – lustful thoughts, anger, and self-serving interests. It was as if I could see within me what the Lord sees.

> *But a man must examine himself, and in so doing he is to*
> *eat of the bread and drink of the cup. (1 Corinthians 11:28)*

This sense has profoundly deepened what the Lord's Supper means to me. I experience it every time I take communion.

Examine thyself. I believe this speaks not only of confession to God, but also an open and honest look at ourselves. The Psalmist's plea must be ours:

> *"Oh, Lord, don't let the hidden faults in my heart control me.*
> *I want the meditation of my heart to be pleasing to You, my*
> *ROCK and my redeemer." (Psalm 19:13)*

I've moved many times in my life, and I've helped many others move. When those I'm helping to move comment about all the junk they have, I'll reply, "You know, the stuff we own ends up owning us!" This is at the heart of the issue of what exists in the heart of man, that the stuff within our heart can own us if we aren't renewing our heart with the Word of God. Again, Proverbs 4:23:

> *"Above all else, guard your heart, for everything you do flows*
> *from it." Proverbs 4:23*

What We House in our Heart

I offer the following insight from a book by Frances Frangipane titled '*The Three Battlegrounds.*'

"The steady stream of information and experience that continually shaped our childhood perceptions is the greatest source of strongholds within us. The amount of love (or lack of love) in our home, our cultural environment, peer values and pressures, as well as fears of rejection and exposure - even our

physical appearance and intelligence, all combine to form our sense of identity and our view of life."

In the excerpt above, the author speaks of strongholds within us - those areas of familiar sins. Those strongholds are territory within us that we have once yielded to the devil, and Satan is jealous to maintain hold of those areas, or to reclaim them as his own.

Again, the author states "A Demonic stronghold is any type of thinking that exalts itself above the knowledge of God, thereby giving the devil a secure place of influence in an individual's thought-life."

We're not to conform to what or who we think we are, or to the likeness of another. Our goal must be conformity to Jesus Christ and Him only. Any lesser thing that does not support this singular purpose must not be allowed to rule us.

Let's look at how we have gone about filling our hearts with what exists within it.

How I went about filling my heart - Pornography

> *"For this is the will of God, your sanctification; that is, that you abstain from sexual immorality that each of you know how to possess his own vessel in sanctification and honor, not in lustful passion, like the Gentiles who do not know God; and that no man transgress and defraud his brother in the matter because the Lord is the avenger in all these things, just as we also told you before and solemnly warned you."*
> *(1 Thessalonians 4:3-6)*

I offer the following personal example of what filled my heart early in my life.

Even as a young boy, I was girl crazy. I still recall the face and name of a girl I was especially fond of in kindergarten. As a sixth grader a few years later, while going through a dresser drawer of my father's, I found a certain magazine. It was new and news to me. I snuck back into my bedroom with it and began to slowly turn the pages. As I did, something raced in me that didn't have wheels. I was enthralled by the images I saw, even shocked, but it excited me in a way no girl had to this point.

I'm not sure how my dad knew that I had his magazine, but I recall him coming into my room and asking me about it, and then following him back into his bedroom and watching as he slowly opened the bottom drawer of his dresser and placing the magazine there. And, to my surprise, there were others there as well - a small stack of them. My father did not attempt to hide anything. When he looked at me, it was as if he gave me silent permission to access them.

Over the months ahead, I became bolder about my interest in those magazines, even to the point of removing the center-folds and tacking them on my bedroom wall. Oddly enough, I was never asked to remove them.

I did not know at the time what I was storing up in my heart. This was the beginning of many years of enslavement to, and a struggle with, pornography. After becoming a follower of Jesus Christ, I continued to battle with pornography, even when I hadn't consciously opened that door to the enemy, or granted permission for myself to do so. I simply chose to view it. There have been times, even in prayer, where it is as if a rolodex of images comes to mind; those images that many years earlier were chemically-etched into my mind. There is science that supports this.

Years later, while in Christian counseling with a few other men on the very subject, it was shown to me that the draw to pornography was my "drug of choice" for the pain I was feeling, and throughout my life I have known a great deal of pain.

As I matured in Christ, the stumbles I experienced with porn became fewer and fewer, but make no mistake - the temptation remains. In the least likely moments, a thought or an image will present itself to me. I no longer wonder to myself "where did that come from?" I know it's the enemy and my old nature that brought it to mind because there's that place within me, from deep within my own heart, where those thoughts and images once held rule and reign in my life.

The devil wants us to entertain the thought and the images because he knows of the potential effect it has on any man, Christian or otherwise. Every time I have spoken on the subject of pornography to other men, it is as if it becomes open season on me in that arena. I have learned to anticipate this. Satan wants to rob me of my testimony. He wants to shame me into silence. He wants to do the same in all of our lives.

> *"… for where your treasure is, there your heart will be also."*
> *(Matthew 6:21)*

What do you treasure?

We must not allow Satan to rob us of our testimonies of the faithfulness and goodness of our Lord in our lives. We must stand firm.

Filling that God-shaped Vacuum

I offer an example of this - of my wanting to place something other than God into the vacuum within me that only He can fill. Several years before I came to faith in Jesus Christ, I thought what truly was missing in my life was a woman, that one woman - a wife.

What I am about to share began in the summer of 1976. I had just finished working in a casino in Lake Tahoe; quite an adventure. I was driving a nice Buick (thanks to my dad), and had a new surfboard strapped to its top. I had planned to leave Lake Tahoe and head to Los Angeles to move in with a buddy, and a job that awaited me there, but there was a hurricane off the Mexican coast and a great swell was breaking all along the southern California coastline, so I drove south from LA towards the Mexican border.

At that time in my life I thought I had the world by the tail. That very morning I thought to myself, "Man, if I died today I could say I've had a good life" (as if that were enough).

After a great day surfing, and later while parked on a beach south of San Clemente, a young couple walked past my car and then northward together up the coast. I watched them for a while as they walked hand in hand.

In the unexpected quiet of that moment, I began to weep. Something seemed to have dawned on me. I hadn't sought out this "truth" - that, indeed, something was missing in my life.

For all I seen and done, for all I had experienced and thought and wrote and witnessed, what was the value of any of it if I had no one to share it with. I felt so alone. I sat in my car for a long time weeping, overcome by that inner sense of loneliness I had worked so hard to deny.

Initially, I didn't know why the tears. In spite of all that I had experienced up to that point, my life suddenly seemed meaningless. Immediately I fired up my car and headed back to Houston to meet and marry a Texas woman, as if that was what was missing in my life.

I did not know that that special someone to share my life with was Jesus Christ, because I did not know Him at the time.

I did meet up with and married that Texas woman, but she did not fill the God-shaped vacuum in my heart. Matter of fact, both of us being non-believers at the time, I didn't know that such a vacuum existed. Yes, we enjoyed many good times, but there was never a true union. In spite of the unspeakable joy of becoming a father to two precious, beautiful, and intelligent daughters, Sarah and Micah, it was a difficult, draining, and troubled marriage that ended painfully after 23 years.

In the garden of Eden, Adam chose Eve over God. We men, all too often, do the same.

Know this, when I state the above, I am not speaking only to single men. Woefully, many married men desire an Eve that they are not married to.

I know several single Christian men (as I am now) who so long to be married that this desire is the one all-compelling drive in their lives. It owns them and I understand that all too well.

Brothers, we tend to fill our hearts with the things we think will bring relief to whatever we are experiencing. In reality, what we are doing is trying to fill the God-shaped vacuum within us that only He can fill.

God is jealous for us. When we seek to fill ourselves with anything other than God, we are committing spiritual adultery against Him. Yes, God gave us free will and He allows us to exercise it. He'll not force anyone's hand.

> *"The God who made the world and all things in it, since He is Lord of heaven and earth, does not dwell in temples made with hands; nor is He served by human hands, as though He needed anything, since He Himself gives to all people life and breath and all things;" (Acts 17:24-25)*

I've shared what I have in the hope that you will give heartfelt consideration to what your heart houses and why. I shared the previous story that you might consider deeply how you have attempted to fill that God-shaped vacuum within you. My prayer is that you will consider your past so as to better understand what exists in your heart - the good, the bad, and the ugly in it.

The Woundedness Within Us

The origins of the woundedness we experience or have experienced can come from any number of external elements. Family or background, interpersonal struggles, the ways we were related to as a child, hardships we have known, etc. can, in part, constitute those areas of deep woundedness within us.

John Eldredge, in his exceptional book, '*Wild at Heart*,' writes this about the wounds we have each known as men, especially during our younger years:

"One thing about the assault wounds – they are obvious. The passive wounds (i.e. ugly words spoken to use in our youth; a father's indifference, etc.) are not; they are pernicious (having a harmful effect, especially in a gradual or subtle way) *like a cancer. Because they are subtle, they often go unrecognized as wounds and therefore are actually more difficult to heal."*

We will look at the power of words, the words we speak and the words spoken to us, in chapter 4.

The issue of woundedness is not my purpose in writing this book, as there are a number of excellent books and/or biblically-based online articles on the subject, but I will address briefly three areas of woundedness that seem to top the ever-growing list of the wounds we Christian men have known in our lives - divorce, loneliness, and what is referred to as the father wound.

Divorce

> *"For this reason a man shall leave his father and his mother,*
> *and be joined to his wife; and they shall become one flesh."*
> *(Genesis 2:24, and also referenced in Matthew 19:5, Mark*
> *10:7-8, and Ephesians 5:31)*

I heard someone once make an interesting comment, saying "there's an ache in the side of Adam until Eve returns to his side - to the very place where Adam's rib was removed; from which she was formed." This speaks to me of the great wounding that one experiences through divorce when the two who have become one are torn apart

Divorce is an incredibly wounding experience. The Word of God says when the two become one, as man and wife, they become one flesh. When a divorce occurs, the two that became one are torn apart. There is a great tearing of our flesh, physically, emotionally, and spiritually. And rather than take the pain to the LORD, we can so quickly strive to patch over the wound by whatever means we may choose. We can so easily default to our old ways, our old nature, in dealing with deep pain.

Tragically, the deep and terrible wound of divorce is often not given the time to heal properly. We, as men, tend to not seek council. We may quickly isolate ourselves or invest ourselves in any number of distractions.

As men, we are often quick to look for another woman, or to alcohol, or we may withdraw from others - even to pornography or worse. We soothe the pain we are experiencing with any number of false substitutes. The options for this false-filling are limitless.

Wounds fester over time. Any medical professional will tell a patient they have examined if there is a source of infection in them and the infection, not the symptom, needs to be treated. The symptom of physical infection may be high fever, high white cell count, swelling and/or soreness, etc., but there is always something more serious behind it. All too often we men choose to deal with the symptoms, rather than the actual cause of the infection.

I had a nurse friend once tell me of a male patient that came into the hospital where she worked, and he was in terrible shape. There were enlarged red and swollen areas on his legs that needed to be opened. Upon the doctor doing so, she said the entire floor of that hospital was overrun with a terrible putrid smell. It was all they could do to clear the air. Just like that man's wound, our wound MUST also be reopened before true healing can even be considered.

There must be a point in our lives when we finally prostrate ourselves before the Lord - when we bring to Him the pain and hurt that is buried deep within us. We must trust God with His scalpel and lie still before Him as we allow Him to reopen the wound within us. It is only then that true healing can begin.

Healing takes time.

Loneliness

About five years into my walk with Jesus I was asked by the church I was attending to speak with the singles department. I was asked to speak on the subject of loneliness. I do not recall all that I shared that evening, but I do remember saying this: "I know that there exists within most of you here the great desire to be married, no doubt. But take your time and know this: There is no greater loneliness than to wake up one morning married to someone you do not love."

At the time I had no idea how prophetic that statement would prove to be in my life. You see, over time I stopped truly loving my wife.

In Henri J. M. Nouwen's book, '*The Wounded Healer*,' he takes an almost mystic look at our suffering, as one who believes in the spiritual apprehension of truths that are beyond the intellect. In it he suggests that loneliness lends itself to an intense search for the experience of unity and community. He goes so far as to say that we, as Christian care-givers, should embrace our wounds, that indeed we must, for it is through them that we can connect with wounded humanity on common grounds. We can articulate our experiences and offer ourselves to others as a source of clarification and truth - clarification about the suffering we all experience in a fallen world.

Regarding suffering and my desire for community I note the following about my life. I have lived in about 45 different physical addresses throughout my life. I went to nine different schools in twelve years during public education. Although I knew and valued many people and had many friendships, the continual relocations that went on in my life made it all but impossible to stay in touch with anyone. No wonder I was so independent prior to coming to faith in Jesus Christ. No wonder I was so lonely.

I've heard it said "to the degree you suffer will you also minister." This is a truth I was slow to embrace, but I recognize and now embrace the truth of it. I think this simple truth summarizes what author Nouwen wrote. He says that we in that we, as caregivers, serve a Moses-like function by articulating our pains and struggles and wounds. In doing so we can lead people out of the land of confusion and alienation and into a land of hope when we invite others to recognize their loneliness on a level where it can, and must be, shared.

When I share some of the struggles I have known in my life with both believers and non-believers, I know that there should be something salty about my speech - that I should speak in such a way that my words might be seasoned so as to be tasty to the hearer. So that it grabs their attention. As a child of the King, I don't want to dwell on the specifics of what I'm suffering, but rather to center my words and focus on the goodness of God during those times. I want my words to be an encouragement and to have impact.

The desire here is that I might be able to state a thing in such a way that it is enjoyable and engaging to listen to. That it might be shared with proper gravity, so that it would impact the other without alerting them to its intent.

I've also heard it said that a burden shared is half a burden. My prayer for us is that we have someone we trust that we can share our struggles and the hurts we've experienced with. Men, we need that someone.

Men, we also need each other because we have all experienced pain. We need to share with other men what we have experienced. Sharing such matters helps to externalize those hurtful memories and feelings from within us. It draws us out of the dark cave of our earlier lives and into the light - the cleansing and healing light of Jesus Christ.

> *Again Jesus spoke to them, saying, "I am the light of the world. Whoever follows me will not walk in darkness, but will have the light of life." (John 8:12)*

If you are struggling with loneliness, the best encouragement I can offer you is not only faithful church attendance, but to also investigate the various Sunday school classes offered. Test the waters. Allow the Spirit of God to lead you and direct you in this.

The Father Wound

As I have grown older I have learned that there are many men, both worldly and Christian, who never experienced the love of their father – nor received their father's blessing. When I hear a man speak about how great his father was, I always tell them how wonderful it is to hear that. Tragically, many women have experienced the same.

As a young boy, the relationship I had with my dad seemed normal until I started visiting my friend's homes. I began to see dads who really seemed to care about their sons in demonstrative ways - they joked and they laughed together. They did stuff together. They'd go outside and toss a ball together. Those fathers went to their sons games and they told their sons "I love you." I heard it spoken.

As a boy and teenager I was considered a natural athlete. In junior high I played football, baseball, and basketball, but my father never attended a single game or practice I ever attended. Not one. Frankly, I don't recall ever having asked him to and I never really noticed his absences.

I had never laughed nor joked with my dad, and until in my early twenties, I do not recall him telling me that he loved me, although I knew he did.

Most men have difficulty expressing their emotions of love and this perpetuates the father wound. Yes, only God can show a father's love. Hearing words of love expressed verbally is extremely important in a man and young boy's life, so the wound is not passed from generation to generation. Simply spoken - "Son, I love you."

Shortly after I became a Christian, and several months before rededicating my life to Christ, I continually lived a defeated life - as if this salvation thing hadn't taken hold with me. I was in church on Sunday and back in Adam, my old nature, the following Monday.

During this period, one night while in prayer, I broke down and confessed to God that I really didn't think I needed Him. I wept aloud as I shamefully confessed this. Then these words came to me; "You've never needed anyone."

As I reflected on those words, I thought about God as being my heavenly Father, only for it to immediately dawn on me that up until that moment, the word father really didn't hold deep meaning to me - indifference at best.

I love my dad and I recognized even as far back as junior high school that he did the best he knew how at the time. I remember and embrace the incredible trips and vacations he took us on - five of us, including my younger twin sisters, Debbie and Denise, in a VW bug as we drove from South Florida to the West Coast, back into the Rocky Mountains, to Indiana to the farm my dad was raised on, then winding our way back to southern Florida, or Oklahoma, or Texas, depending on where we lived at the time.

I hold dear the memories of the many times we played miniature golf as a family and the adventure-filled drives into the Everglades. But my father experienced a very difficult upbringing by his dad, a father who was overly strict and a man who showed little love or grace to my dad or to his brothers. Yes, my father's dad provided for him and his six siblings - they had food, clothing, shelter, but little if any expressions of love.

Several years ago I was asked to give a message at my dad's church - to preach on Father's Day. I was led to share a message about the blessing of the father as spoken by Israel (Jacob) to his sons and by Isaac to his two sons.

About midway thru my message I felt an inner sense that I was to offer an invitation - something that didn't happen at this church – an invitation to anyone who never received a blessing from their father, that I might speak a blessing over them. Much to my surprise, four people came forward. My father was one of the four....

My father had known a father's wound — a deep one as many men have experienced. Men and women need the blessing of hearing their father say to them, "I love you." Again, hearing words of love is extremely important so that the wound is not passed from generation to generation.

Only God can show us a father's love.

Yes, we need a loving father - a loving Heavenly Father.

<u>**The Beauty of Brokenness**</u>

The aforementioned limited sampling of the areas of woundedness in our lives lends itself to a look at brokenness. In the world, broken and damaged goods and people are discarded or thrown away - be they relationships or marriages, you name it. Praise the Lord that God doesn't dispose of us when we're broken. For that matter, God delights in our brokenness. Our brokenness brings us closer to God. Brokenness is a prerequisite in a man's life before God can begin to use him for His purposes; only then can God actually use us.

We find one of the best biblical portrayals of brokenness in Psalm 51, just after David is outed by the court prophet, Nathan, regarding David's adulterous affair with Bathsheba and his subsequent murder of her husband, Uriah. Hear below the words of a man known as "a man after God's own heart."

> *"Be gracious to me, O God, according to Your lovingkindness; according to the greatness of Your compassion blot out my transgressions. Wash me thoroughly from my iniquity and cleanse me from my sin. For I know my transgressions, and my sin is ever before me. Against You, You only, I have sinned and done what is evil in Your sight, so that You are justified when You speak and blameless when You judge. (Psalm 51:1-4)*

Hide Your face from my sins and blot out all my iniquities. Create in me a clean heart, O God, and renew a steadfast spirit within me. Do not cast me away from Your presence and do not take Your Holy Spirit from me. Restore to me the joy of Your salvation and sustain me with a willing spirit. (Psalm 51:9-12)

For You do not delight in sacrifice, otherwise I would give it; You are not pleased with burnt offering. The sacrifices of God are a broken spirit; a broken and a contrite heart, O God, You will not despise." (Psalm 51:16-17)

How might David have felt upon hearing Nathan's words about his sin? What physical or emotional signs of brokenness might he have displayed? Try to see this in your mind's eye as if you were Nathan. (Read 2 Samuel 12:1-17 to help better set the stage for your understanding of this.)

Brokenness! That's what happened to David - deep, sincere brokenness.

Interesting, no sooner had I written the above, a memory came to me about a time when I was on staff at a church in the Pacific Northwest. It was on a Sunday and I had just finished teaching a large class of some 60 people on what we as a church believed. Upon closing in prayer, I quickly hurried to the kitchen where the communion trays awaited my filling. I was exhausted!

As I quickly and carefully went about the work, a young man walked past the open counter and saw me working. I don't know why he said what he did, but he spoke this. "Ah, one of the Lord's vessels at work."

I smiled and half-looking up, replied, "Yeah, a broken vessel," and I truly felt that at that moment. He responded, "A broken vessel is the only vessel God can use." I now understand and embrace what he meant.

May our heart and prayer be, "Break me, Lord!"

God does not want Christian men to try to pick themselves up by their own strength and by their own bootstraps and try, try again. Brokenness produces humility in the heart of a person. It breaks us of the pride in our heart and our spirit. When we are broken, we begin to take on the image of Christ. Our brokenness makes us more like Jesus.

> *"The Lord is near to the brokenhearted and saves those who are crushed in spirit." (Psalm 34:18)*

> *"Make me to hear joy and gladness, let the bones which You have broken rejoice." (Psalm 51:8)*

> *"He heals the brokenhearted and binds up their wounds." (Psalm 147:3)*

Psalm 147:3 has a special meaning for me - I smile as I write this. I once had a 20-mile commute to work. Most of it was on a north/south-bound freeway. Halfway into the commute I'd pass an exit where a so-called men's club was - it was called Heart-Breakers.

I had been a Christian for only about two years at the time and had a real fervor and passion for the Lord. Nothing excited me more than seeing or hearing of others coming to faith in Jesus Christ. So every time I'd pass that club, I'd lift my hand in prayer for both the dear ladies that worked there and for the men that frequented the place. There was almost a heaviness I could sometimes feel as I passed the place.

One Monday morning as I was driving south to work, as I neared this men's club, I lifted my right hand and began to pray. As I was about to pass it, I took my eyes off the road and looked to my right at the club.

Wow! Over the weekend, a new and larger billboard had been erected adjacent to the club. Praise broke out on Interstate 45 as I read, "He heals the broken-hearted!" (Psalm 147:3)

A Personal Word on Brokenness

During a period in my walk with the Lord, I wanted to learn more about the redemptive power of brokenness - I wanted a greater understanding about it in my own life. I read several books on the subject. One of the books was by Gene Edwards titled, '*The Tale of Three Kings.*' After reading his work, I noted the following in my journal:

"On March 9th, 1983, I enrolled in God's school of brokenness. That was the night I rededicated my life to God. I was serious about my rededication. So was the Lord. Brokenness 101! So tough was the course that it was several years later before I realized that I was not the only one enrolled in it.

I became an insulin-dependent type 1 diabetic during that time. So marked and abrupt was the brokenness schooling. I knew there had to be a reason for the piling on of events and circumstances and for the trials and the surprises, and the pain. I knew NOT the reasons, though I labored to understand them. God knew - only He wasn't telling. It is, indeed, a difficult truth to reconcile – that God greatly desires men who would live in pain, or at least those who are willing to do so."

While in the Midst of Brokenness

It is very difficult to share anything redemptive about suffering and brokenness when you're smack-dab in the middle of it. Any attempt to do so would be akin to taking a large, hard, bitter green apple and offering a bite to everyone present. There would be no joy in it. It would be hard, bitter, taste sour, and bring an ache to the stomach.

Shortly after rededicating my life to Christ, a well-meaning friend and member of our small group asked me to share about the redemptive suffering in my life. All those present knew of it. Upon being asked, I simply broke down and wept. No words came forth. The redemptive suffering was ongoing at the time.

I later shared with my friend that there will come a day, in the Lord's timetable for such, where the redemptive brokenness in my life would have a fragrant, juicy, sweet, and pleasing taste the Lord foresaw it to be all about. We embraced each other at the thought.

I have found in my life that the same suffering that kills the man also gives birth to humility. I have learned this about broken men. One of the things brokenness breaks us of is our pride.

Broken men talk less and love God more.

One Thursday evening while at small men's weekly gathering, a new guy was present. I did not know him. Halfway into the evening he asked me, "What is brokenness?" I saw it all over him. He had earlier acknowledged an unspoken concern, something deep within him that he desired to keep in the dark (not his words).

I shared with him the green apple analogy. His eyes watered as I recalled the bleakness of those despairing earlier days in my life. I knew at that time in my life *(and to this day)* that it was all about surrender and submission of my life, and the Spirit whispered to me then that it was the same for my new friend.

I encouraged him to let God have His way in his life - to submit to what He was doing and wanting to do, and to trust Him as he draws closer to God. Yes, it sounds so easy....

To me, '*The Tale of Three Kings*' was about submission and authority in and to the Kingdom of God. This is the gem that the heat and the pressure of the brokenness process creates in a man - a man submitted to the process and committed to the Lord who calls him into it.

King David never feared being dethroned because he fully recognized and embraced the sovereignty of God. I am most impressed with this aspect of David. I pray that I will someday take full hold of this sentiment in regards to the new life I live in Jesus Christ, even with all of its challenges, trials, and struggles.

Study Guide - Chapter 2

Day 1

a) What's your heartfelt response to the below passage?

b) Why might you (we) struggle to embrace it?

"The heart is more deceitful than all else and is desperately sick; who can understand it?" (Jeremiah 17:9)

Response:

c) In this chapter there is the following quote: "The steady stream of information and experience that continually shaped our childhood perceptions is the greatest source of strongholds within us." In light of this, what stronghold might there be in you, in your heart, that needs to be addressed and overcome?

d) How were these strongholds established?

Responses:

Day 2

a) With what things have you attempted to fill that God-shaped vacuum within you?

b) Of them, which remains a challenge for you to put to death?

c) We have all experienced hurt, pain, disappointment, and brokenness in our lives. Prayerfully consider what you have experienced that most readily comes to mind; the deepest hurts. Be honest with yourself.

d) List a few of the most painful below. Externalize them, and then offer them to the Lord. Give them to Him!

Responses:

Day 3

a) How would you summarize your relationship with your earthly father?
b) What kind of dad was he to you? What brought you the most meaning or joy?
c) What hurt you the most?

Responses:

d) Ask yourself these two questions: "Who am I and why am I here?" In the space provided below, take a shot at answering these two questions of yourself.

Responses:

Day 4

a) How you known brokenness? Have you been broken? Briefly capture what you can of the process you went through; what you felt while in the midst of it; what those spiritually defining moments in your life were all about.
b) Are you, today, in the process of brokenness? Write about it; allow it to come to the surface.

Responses:

Day 5

Read and briefly comment on each of the following scriptural passages. Make note of the encouragement and strength you find in them; personalize them; respond to the Lord.

Passage: *"Search me, O God, and know my heart; try me and know my anxious thoughts; and see if there be any hurtful way in me, and lead me in the everlasting way." (Psalm 139:23-24)*

Response:

Passage: *"Set a guard, O Lord, over my mouth; keep watch over the door of my liPsalm Do not incline my heart to any evil thing, to practice deeds of wickedness with men who do iniquity; and do not let me eat of their delicacies." (Psalm 141:3-4)*

Response:

Passage: *"Teach me Your way, O Lord; I will walk in Your truth; unite my heart to fear Your name. I will give thanks to You, O Lord my God, with all my heart, and will glorify Your name forever. For Your lovingkindness toward me is great, and You have delivered my soul from the depths of Sheol." (Psalm 86:11-13)*

Response:

Passage: *"Moreover, I will give you a new heart and put a new spirit within you; and I will remove the heart of stone from your flesh and give you a heart of flesh." (Ezekiel 36:26)*

The New Living Translation words it this way:

And I will give you a new heart, and I will put a new spirit in you. I will take out your stony, stubborn heart and give you a tender, responsive heart. (Ezekiel 36:26; NLT)

Response:

Chapter 3

THE MIND OF MAN

"Set your minds on things above, not on earthly things. For you died, and your life is now hidden with Christ in God. When Christ, who is your life, appears, then you also will appear with him in glory. Put to death, therefore, whatever belongs to your earthly nature: sexual immorality, impurity, lust, evil desires and greed, which is idolatry." (Colossians 3:2-5)

What the Mind of Man Dwells On

We've taken a look at the heart of man so as to see and better understand what that warehouse of information within us is comprised of. It's the source from which the minds of men draw upon - we do so as if unconsciously. Now we'll take a look at our minds.

> *"For the mind set on the flesh is death, but the mind set on the Spirit is life and peace, because the mind set on the flesh is hostile toward God; for it does not subject itself to the law of God, for it is not even able to do so, and those who are in the flesh cannot please God." (Romans 8:6-8)*

What a powerful passage - "For the mind set on the flesh is death… and those who are in the flesh cannot please God." I encourage you to re-read the passage.

Again, our flesh wants to be god.

Our Self-Worshipping Nature

We, by nature, are self-worshipping. The old nature we struggle with is a construct of all we have believed in and held dear in our lives prior to coming to faith in Jesus Christ.

Even beyond that salvation moment, we can so easily lapse back into the former ways thinking and behaving. It's akin to fogging our home to rid us of the roaches, only to leave the doors and windows open and scattered crumbs on the counter as if to invite them all back in.

Someone once asked me what I hated. There were several responses I considered, but at the heart of it was this: "I hate this stinking flesh!" The sinful struggle in my mind came from the ground I had surrendered in my heart to the enemy. The heart is where those thoughts and images reside.

You know, I never gave any consideration to surrendering pieces of my heart to the enemy as I was growing up. It is like a form of drug abuse or cancer. Trust me, I should know. What we feed upon ends up feeding on us. What got you high one day soon required twice as much for the same effect. Sin works in a similar manner - ever escalating.

> *The longer we remain in the grip of sinful ways, in whatever form, the more distant thoughts of God become.*

We are driven by the thoughts and feelings we have and entertain. To be driven implies being led in a given direction. What directions have your thoughts or feelings driven you to lately?

Unchecked fantasies, thoughts, or imaginings can easily take a foothold in our mind. They must be judged or evaluated immediately. Sexual feelings and romantic attractions are normal and healthy gifts from God, but entertained and prolonged sexual thoughts or the revisit of suggestive materials and images are against the very nature of God and violate all Biblical standards.

If such thoughts or imaginings are not dealt with immediately, they will take on a life of their own. They will grieve the Holy Spirit of God within us and greatly hinder our relationship with the Lord. Satan wants Christian men and women to become POW's (prisoners of war) to whatever enslaves us, so as to remove us from the fight.

Again, giving into Satan's temptations can separate us from the things of God. A thought can come like an uninvited guest. Although Satan may beat on the door of our mind, we don't have to open it, or ourselves, to him. Ask Jesus to answer the door.

I propose to you that our heart holds our deepest desires and our mind is comprised of the means or methods by which we seek to satisfy what the heart holds dear.

My brother, the battleground for the Christian man is the mind, and the mind dwells on the things that already exist in the heart. The Word of God says that our minds must be renewed.

> *Therefore I urge you, brethren, by the mercies of God, to present your bodies a living and holy sacrifice, acceptable to God, which is your spiritual service of worship. And do not be conformed to this world, but be transformed by the renewing of your mind, so that you may prove what the will of God is, that which is good and acceptable and perfect. (Romans 12:1-2)*

God is more interested in what we do with these sinful thoughts than the thoughts themselves.

Our Need for Spiritual Renewal

Our need for renewal begins with the intentional reading and study of the Word of God. Our old nature - that corrupt database within us (our old nature) - is the one that's set up to make our flesh god, and it needs to be overwritten with His Word. We must be intentional about devoting ourselves to reading, studying, and meditating upon the Word of God.

We must be about filling our mind with Scripture so that at the moment of attack we have the Word of God to speak to the spiritual assault - however it is made manifest to us. We must study the Word of God so that the Holy Spirit of God can bring a Scripture or passage to mind when it's needed. We've got to give the indwelling Holy Spirit of God something to work with.

Jesus knew the Word (He is the Word - read John 1:1 and 4) and responded with the Word of God when Satan sought to tempt Him. Let's look at this account as given in Luke 4:1-13 which says this: Verses 1-4:

> *Jesus, full of the Holy Spirit, returned from the Jordan and was led around by the Spirit in the wilderness for forty days, being tempted by the devil. And He ate nothing during those days, and when they had ended, He became hungry. And the devil said to Him, "If You are the Son of God, tell this stone to become bread." And Jesus answered him, "It is written, 'Man shall not live on bread alone.'" (Luke 4:1-4)*

No doubt, the Lord was hungry. I'd be so after only forty hours. The point here is: Satan targets us when we are weak and tired. Luke 4:5-8:

> *And he led Him up and showed Him all the kingdoms of the world in a moment of time. And the devil said to Him, "I will give You all this domain and its glory; for it has been handed over to me, and I give it to whomever I wish. Therefore if You worship before me, it shall all be Yours." Jesus answered him, "It is written, 'You shall worship the Lord your God and serve Him only.'" (Luke 4:5-8)*

Satan wants to be worshipped. This passage speaks of taking the easy way – selling out. However, Jesus purposed in eternity past that the kingdoms of this world be His – by way of the cross. Jesus responds, "Worship God only." Luke 4:9-12:

> *And he led Him to Jerusalem and had Him stand on the pinnacle of the temple, and said to Him, "If You are the Son*

> *of God, throw Yourself down from here; for it is written, 'He*
> *will command His angels concerning You to guard You,' and,*
> *'On their hands they will bear You up, So that You will not*
> *strike Your foot against a stone.'" And Jesus answered and*
> *said to him, "It is said, 'You shall not put the Lord your God*
> *to the test.'" (Luke 4:9-12)*

Satan here tempts Jesus to prove His divinity. "Do something spectacular! Prove you are the Son of God!" Jesus replies there is nothing He has to prove. His will was to do the will of His father in Heaven. Luke 4:13:

> *When the devil had finished every temptation, he left Him*
> *until an opportune time. (Luke 4:13)*

Although the biblical record does not speak of any other verbal attack upon Jesus by Satan, Satan did continue to assault Him. He attacked Jesus Christ through others, like the religious rulers, even to the point that they accused Him of being demon-possessed – that He was performing the miracles He did through the power of Satan.

He was assaulted by disbelief from the very people He spoke to daily and came to give His life for - those nearest to Him, His own people (the Hebrew nation), His own family, even His slow-minded disciples.

The Overcoming Power of the Word of God

Satan also attacked the words of Jesus by closing the ears of the many who heard Him speak. They rejected Him and His Word. See parallel passages of this as noted in gospels of Matthew (chapter 13), Mark (chapter 4), and Luke (chapter 8); the parable of the sower and Jesus' explanation of this parable to His disciples - to those slow to believe themselves. Satan blinds the eyes and deafens the ears of those who hear the gospel today. I've seen it happen, likely you have, too.

> *"So will My word be which goes forth from My mouth; it*
> *will not return to Me empty, without accomplishing what I*

> *desire, and without succeeding in the matter for which I sent it." (Isaiah 55:11)*

Praise God that His Word does not return void! His Word must be proclaimed and we must know His Word to do so.

In the Luke 4:1-13 passages on the temptations of Jesus Christ, Satan's three temptations posed upon Jesus were:

1. Satan said to Jesus "you're hungry – make bread" (verse 4:3)
2. After showing Jesus all the kingdoms of the world, Satan arrogantly said "worship me and all of these things shall be yours." (verses 4:5-7
3. Lastly, Satan tempted Jesus to do something amazing so as to call attention to Himself. (verses 4:9-11)

All three times that Jesus was tempted by Satan, He spoke the Word of God to the tempter. In doing so, He silenced His oppressor.

The Three Temptations Satan levied to Jesus...

1. Jesus didn't need to make bread. His bread was to do the will of the Father. And, as wonderfully noted in the gospel of John 6:38, Jesus declared himself to be the bread of life.
2. The kingdoms of the world were Satan's to offer, but Jesus was going to secure them to himself by way of the cross.
3. When Satan tempted Jesus the third time, he even used scripture in response to Jesus Christ, but Jesus came to do the will of His Father. The attention He would draw to himself would come... on the cross.

In the Luke 14:1-13 verses, I want to draw extra emphasis on verse 13; *"When the devil had finished every temptation, he left Him **until an opportune time**."* (Emphasis added.)

We must be ever vigilant - 24/7. Praise God, we will experience victory over the temptations levied against us as we take every thought captive to

Christ. For us to take captive every thought to Christ (2 Corinthians 10:5) has to be simultaneous with one's awareness of the thought's presence. But know this, the enemy of God and of our souls will do with us as he did with Jesus. He'll revisit us at a later date - at a more opportune time.

In our day to day walk with our Lord and risen Savior, we will be assaulted. Sometimes it is as if attacks upon us are relentless, but there will also be periods of relative peace.

I heard Adrian Rogers ask once on the radio, "Is there a 'wanted' poster of you in Satan's post office?" I smiled broadly hearing that, both now and then. The thing he was asking is "are we on Satan's radar?"

I once worked in the space and defense arm of a large company on the West Coast. One of our team's was called IFF - Identify Friend or Foe. At the time, I hadn't made the spiritual connection of that team's title with what I heard Adrian Rogers later ask, but I do now. If we are a friend of Christ, then rest assured - we are the enemy of Satan. He sees us as a foe!

Are you on Satan's Radar?

Satan's assaults are varied in nature. There may be periods in our life where we may not be as aware of our enemy, but know this: just as Satan left Jesus until an opportune time, he'll do so in our lives as well. By the power and strength of the indwelling Holy Spirit, let's not open the door to that opportunity. Again, simply put - when Satan knocks, don't answer.

Once our mind grows accustomed to darkened enticement, the only way to renew the light within us is through the Word of God. Colossians 3:2 admonishes us to *"set your mind on the things above, not on the things that are on earth."*

Knowing, memorizing, and treasuring the Word of God in our hearts is the greatest renewal component of a life being transformed by Jesus Christ.

Jesus is the Living Word - His Word must live in us.

Renewal can only happen when we submit ourselves to the reading and study of God's Word and to the leading of His indwelling Holy Spirit within us, but this takes an act of the will, our will, to do so. We must be ever vigilant to the fact that we have an internal library of ideas, thoughts, experiences, desires, and the like that want to download into the present experience of our lives.

Again, we must take our thoughts captive to Christ and recognize that our failing to do so will only lead us to repeat past failures and, once again, to fall into that dark cycle of revisited sin and the daunting sense of shame that always follows.

<u>Renewing the Mind</u>

In that first critical moment of temptation how is the Holy Spirit going to bring to your mind a Biblical passage if you have not first made a practice of reading the Word? We must read the Word, make a study of it, talk about it, reflect upon on, and treasure it.

The renewing of our mind is about introducing into our mind, and thus our heart, that something superior to what we have housed in our hearts and minds all of our lives. Each time we choose to replace a sinful desire, motive, attitude or thought with a biblical one, we are in the process of being renewed - transformed.

> *"Therefore we do not lose heart, but though our outer man is decaying, yet our inner man is being renewed day by day. For momentary, light affliction is producing for us an eternal weight of glory far beyond all comparison, while we look not at the things which are seen, but at the things which are not seen; for the things which are seen are temporal, but the things which are not seen are eternal." (2 Corinthians 4:16-18)*

As we invest ourselves in the Word of God, the Bible says we are being renewed day by day. Merriam-Webster defines invest as, "to make use of for future benefits or advantage; to involve or engage especially emotionally." These two definitions speak to our investing ourselves in the reading, the studying, and the memorization of the Word of God.

Likely you've heard the expression garbage in – garbage out. In our lives before Christ, it was garbage in all the time. We took into our hearts data through our experiences, our impressions, our emotions and feelings, the words spoken to us, the words not spoken to us, etc. Because we house an overload of garbage, it is only natural that garbage out must happen.

> *"You were taught, with regard to your former way of life, to put off your old self, which is being corrupted by its deceitful desires; to be made new in the attitude of your minds; and to put on the new self, created to be like God in true righteousness and holiness." (Ephesians 4:22-24)*

Because what is in our heart is what we draw upon to make sense of our world, an ongoing and lifelong infilling of the Word of God is needed in order to overwrite our past data dumps. It's a matter of out with the old and in with the new, and the only way we can invest as much as is needed for our future advantage is by reading, studying, and reflecting upon God's Word.

Susan Thomas, an author at Association of Biblical Counselors makes these tremendous comments regarding our thought life:

"The battle for our thoughts is no doubt a reality and crucial to the victorious life of every individual. Taking our thoughts captive and making them obedient to God is a vital practice in the life of every Christ follower. But, if we stop there, I believe we have missed THE ROOT of our struggle. You see, behind every errant thought, there is a heart problem."

Behind every errant thought, there is a heart problem.

She continues: *"Now I'm not talking necessarily about the errant thoughts that pop in your head and you instantly dismiss. I'm really not even talking about thoughts of temptation. I'm talking about the thoughts that linger. The thoughts that we entertain. The thoughts that can turn into beliefs. We must understand that something drives our thoughts! We have a nature, a heart condition that actively influences our thought life. The desires inside our hearts lure and entice us. Out of our hearts, thoughts flow! And because we have a heart condition that is either very, very sick or being healed by our Savior, we must take seriously the state of our hearts."*

Those who are dominated by the sinful nature think about sinful things, but those who are controlled by the Holy Spirit think about things that please the Spirit. (Romans 8:5, NLT)

For from the heart come evil thoughts… (Matthew 15:19a, NLT)

Out of our hearts, come the thoughts that we think! Our hearts are full of all kinds of desires, and our desires are often expressed via our thoughts. While intricately connected, we must understand that the condition of our heart directly impacts the nature of our thought life. If we are dominated by our sinful nature and heart, then our thoughts will set out to destroy us and all God loves. If we are controlled by the Holy Spirit of God, our thoughts will bring life and joy to our existence and even to the lives of those around us!"

Susan Thomas closes by stating:

"It means that no amount of effort or thought control will ever be enough when it comes to the problems I face in my life. Controlling our thought life is important. But we must get first things first. We must love God. When I love God, I will obey him. When I run to Jesus, my thought life will follow."

———————————————

There is an excellent passage that speaks soundly about the repopulation of that corrupt database (our self-worshipping minds) and the heart within each of us. Our heart, the database within us, must be replenished with new data to draw upon; the Word of God. The Philippians passage below so wonderfully expresses this.

"Finally, brothers and sisters, whatever is true, whatever is noble, whatever is right, whatever is pure, whatever is lovely, whatever is admirable—if anything is excellent or praiseworthy—think about such things." (Philippians 4:8)

I treasure this passage. I have this verse taped above my computer in my bedroom. Every quality mentioned speaks directly to what the Word of God is. It is true, honorable, just, pure, lovely, commendable, and excellent. Jesus Christ is each of these qualities and only Jesus Christ is worthy of our praise.

If we're left to our own strength, we'll fail miserably in this. Everything in the physical world around us wants to draw us in the opposite direction, to take us back to that dark cave we once existed in. Again, be on the alert – our flesh wants to be god.

"Therefore if anyone is in Christ, he is a new creature; the old things passed away; behold, new things have come." (2 Corinthians 5:17)

The Word tells us that the second we gave our hearts and lives to Jesus - the moment we embraced Him as risen Savior and Lord - all that we are in Christ is given to us. Men, we are now new creations.

A new nature has been given to us, but it is only by the indwelling Holy Spirit of God can we even begin to incorporate our new nature into our daily experience. We are to be engaged in this transformation process unto the second we awake at the feet of Jesus.

"but like the Holy One who called you, be holy yourselves also in all your behavior; because it is written, "You shall be holy, for I am holy." (1 Peter 1:15-16)

While we remain on this fallen earth, we are called to be holy - holy in our thoughts, our words, our deeds, and in our behavior. That call to holiness is an incredible call upon each of us, and there can only be that transformation - the call to holiness - in Jesus Christ.

> *And the four living creatures, each one of them having six wings, are full of eyes around and within; and day and night they do not cease to say, "HOLY, HOLY, HOLY is THE LORD GOD, THE ALMIGHTY, WHO WAS AND WHO IS AND WHO IS TO COME." (Revelation 4:8)*

Holy is one of only two words in the Word of God used three times in a single verse. My sense of this is that each use of the word "Holy" references each personality of our triune God: God the Father, God the Son, and God the Holy Spirit. (We'll look at the other word, woe, in chapter 6.)

> *"if indeed you have heard Him and have been taught in Him, just as truth is in Jesus, that, in reference to your former manner of life, you lay aside the old self [put off], which is being corrupted in accordance with the lusts of deceit, and that you be renewed in the spirit of your mind, and put on the new self, which in the likeness of God has been created in righteousness and holiness of the truth." (Ephesians 4:21-24)*

Simple truth - putting on entails taking off. If we are the ones who are to put on the good and godly qualities that God wants us to have operating in our lives, we are to put off the corrupt stuff - all of the bad and negative qualities that God doesn't want operating in our being and in our lives. The Word of God is the live ammunition we must draw upon in our day to day battles. Psalms 26:2 needs to be our prayer:

> **"Examine me, O Lord, and try me; Test my mind and my heart." (Psalm 26:2)**

We must ask the Holy Spirit of God to examine us from the inside out. The heart and the mind must always be under His leadership. This is the essence of renewal and growth of every Christian man.

Study Guide - Chapter 3

Day 1

a) Read the below passages and then consider your response to this question: What needs to be 'put to death' in your life today?

Passage: *"Set your minds on things above, not on earthly things. For you died, and your life is now hidden with Christ in God. When Christ, who is your life, appears, then you also will appear with him in glory. Put to death, therefore, whatever belongs to your earthly nature: sexual immorality, impurity, lust, evil desires and greed, which is idolatry." (Colossians 3:2-5)*

Response:

b) In this chapter the following was stated: *"We are driven by the thoughts and feelings we have and entertain. To be driven implies being led in a given direction."*

Question: What directions have your thoughts and feelings driven you to in the past? Of late?

Responses:

c) In this chapter it was noted that we, by nature and in our flesh, are self-worshipping. Consider how you may have worshipped self in the past, and then put to pen what you feel may have driven you to self-worship in such a manner. What was lacking in your life at that time?

Responses:

Day 2

Reread the Luke 4:13 passage: "*When the devil had finished every temptation, he left Him until an opportune time.*"

Question:

a) Someone once shared the acronym H.A.L.T. with me. Each of the four letters represents a word, a state of mind, where we can be easily tempted while in. They are Hungry, Angry, Lonely, and Tired. Which of these four states are you most vulnerable in?

b) Given your knowledge about yourself, both before coming to faith in Jesus Christ and since, what might a "more opportune time" look like in your life today? (Point here is to be forewarned is to be forearmed.)

Responses:

Day 3

In reference to Adrian Roger's question; "*Is there a 'wanted' poster of you in Satan's post office?*"

Question:

a) Is there a wanted poster of you in Satan's post office?

b) If so, what might Satan accuse you of on it? What might you be 'wanted' for? Feel free to take some license in your response; aka – have fun with the answer.

Responses:

Day 4

a) Comment on the statement **'Behind every errant thought, there is a heart problem.'**

b) What types of errant thoughts sometimes come to your mind that might point to a heart problem within you?

Responses:

Day 5

Read and briefly comment on each of the following scriptural passages about our minds. Make note of the encouragement and strength you find in them; personalize them; respond to the LORD about them. Ask Him to open your eyes to these passages.

Passage: *"Furthermore, just as they did not think it worthwhile to retain the knowledge of God, so God gave them over to a depraved mind, so that they do what ought not to be done." (Romans 1:28)*

Response:

Passage: *"You were taught, with regard to your former way of life, to put off your old self, which is being corrupted by its deceitful desires; to be made new in the attitude of your minds; and to put on the new self, created to be like God in true righteousness and holiness." (Ephesians 4:22-24)*

Response:

Romans chapter 8 is so very rich. Read the following passages from that chapter and comment to them. What might the Spirit of God be speaking through them to you?

Verses 1-3: *Therefore there is now no condemnation for those who are in Christ Jesus. For the law of the Spirit of life in Christ Jesus has set you free from the law of sin and of death. For what the Law could not do, weak as it was through the flesh, God did: sending His own Son in the likeness of sinful flesh and as an* offering *for sin, He condemned sin in the flesh, (Romans 8:1-3)*

Response:

Verses 4-6: *so that the requirement of the Law might be fulfilled in us, who do not walk according to the flesh but according to the Spirit. For those who are according to the flesh set their minds on the things of the flesh, but those who are according to the Spirit, the things of the Spirit. For the mind set on the flesh is death, but the mind set on the Spirit is life and peace, (Romans 8:4-6)*

Response:

Verses 7-8: *because the mind set on the flesh is hostile toward God; for it does not subject itself to the law of God, for it is not even able* to do so, *and those who are in the flesh cannot please God. (Romans 8:7-8)*

Response:

Chapter 4
ACT LIKE A MAN

"Be on the alert, stand firm in the faith, act like men, be strong" (1 Corinthians 16:13)

What is it to Act Like a True Man?

We've looked at the battle we are in as Christian men. We've taken a look at the heart of man and at our own hearts. We've considered some of the sources of the things that call out to us in a worldly way as Christian men. In chapter 3 we looked at the mind of man – especially focusing on what the Word of God says about it. We also took a look at both what our mind dwells on and why it does what it does.

It is my prayer that each of us have benefited from our look at these things and that we've learned something about ourselves, and the old nature within us, that wants to thwart our forward movement in Jesus Christ and His call on our lives.

Now we will look at what it means to act like a man. I call the man we are to act like a True Man. We'll start by looking at the four interrelated directives given us in the 1 Corinthians 16:13 passage - Be on the Alert - Stand Firm in the Faith - Act like Men - Be Strong.

A True Man Remains on the Alert

> *"**Be on the alert**, stand firm in the faith, act like men, be strong" (1 Corinthians 16:13; emphasis mine)*

When a band of soldiers is moving forward, there is always someone assigned to run point. In modern military terms, to take point, or walk point, or to be on point (point man), means to assume the foremost forward exposed position in a combat military formation. That is, the leading soldier of a unit of men advancing through hostile or unsecured territory assumes responsibility for their forward movement. The phrase can be applied to infantry or mechanized columns as well.

That select soldier leads the men that are following him. He must rely on what he knows about the enemy they are in conflict with. He must know the general direction they are heading as a unit, and he must be on guard for sight or sounds of the enemy's presence - so as to spot them before being spotted by them.

Additionally, when soldiers are in enemy territory and at a temporary halt, someone is always assigned to post guard. The guard is to be eyes and ears for the others as they take rest. The guard typically takes up a position of high ground and finds a spot with an unobstructed view of the area around them.

He watches for movement in the environment around them and he listens for any audible anomaly – the sounds of rustling or movement, or sounds of branches or twigs being broken, for the sound of voices and the like. These soldiers know about the schemes of their enemy because they have history with them. Consider him a watchman. (We'll examine the pivotal role of a watchman in chapter 6.)

The Word of God says that we, too, are to be on guard against the schemes of Satan.

> *"…so that no advantage would be taken of us by Satan, for we are not ignorant of his schemes." (2 Corinthians 2:11)*

Satan's methods, his schemes, haven't changed because his old ones still work. For that matter, he'd just as soon we not believe he exists. However:

> *"Be of sober spirit, be on the alert. Your adversary, the devil, prowls around like a **roaring** lion, seeking someone to devour." (1 Peter 5:8; emphasis mine)*

In this passage, the roaring refers to the prideful, boastful arrogance of Satan, but I have often found in my walk with Christ that Satan sometimes chooses not to roar. He often prefers to be more subtle, even to make his presence felt as a source of excitement or fun. A memory comes to mind in this regard.

While serving in a bus ministry, I had the joy of meeting two precious young South Korean girls - sisters. I first met their parents at a convenience store they owned and ran, and after getting to know them, and they, me, they allowed me to come by their home on Sunday mornings and bring their two daughters to church. I did so for a year or so prior to their parents moving. Before they moved, they gave me their new address.

Several months later, I found myself near their address and thought to drop in on them and see how they were doing. It was summer and I had hoped they'd be home. After knocking on their apartment door I saw the curtains to my right move and a moment later, the door opened. It was a joy for me to see the two of them and they me. I was invited in. There was another young girl there with them - a friend.

I asked how they were and what they'd been up to. The honesty of their immediate response surprised me as they told me they had just finished playing with a Ouija board. All three of their faces showed concern about having done so.

I looked at each of them and then asked, as if led to do so, "How did it make you feel?"

They fidgeted nervously for a moment. "Did it make you feel excited?" I asked. All three heads nodded in the affirmative. The elder sister shared a bit more about it. She then admitted that it also scared her, stating that it 'answered' something that only she knew about.

I told them I understood the excited feelings they experienced, then stating, "It's one of Satan's ploys; one of his sneaky ways."

I pointed to a closed closet door in the room and said "Know this, if Satan was behind this door, we could open it and see him for the truly evil being that he is. No degree of excitement would ever draw us to him."

I shared that the devil will come to us as fun and excitement, but that he hates the three of them and me, as he hates all those who love Jesus Christ.

The three girls listened attentively to everything I shared. Each thanked me for paying them a visit and we hugged. I was so glad I "chose" to drop in that day.

> *"Put on the full armor of God, so that you will be able to stand firm against the schemes of the devil." (Ephesians 6:11)*

We're to be on the alert because there is an enemy that wants to derail us in our walk with the Lord. Satan wants us to act like men as the world defines how men should act.

> ***My brothers, we are to be forceful and passionately intentional about the battle we are in.***

A True Man Stands Firm in the Faith

> *"Be on the alert, **stand firm in the faith**, act like men, be strong" (1 Corinthians 16:13; emphasis mine)*

We are exhorted throughout Scripture to stand firm in our faith. But what does it mean to stand firm? Let's start with a look at a definition of stand firm.

Definition: (verb): refuse to abandon one's opinion or belief

- Synonyms: hold firm, stand fast
- Types: hunker down, to hold stubbornly to a position
- Type of: insist, take a firm stand, be emphatic or resolute and refuse to budge

"Therefore, my brothers, whom I love and long for, my joy and crown, stand firm thus in the Lord, my beloved." (Philippians 4:1)

In an internet-posted article on Philippians 4:1 titled "Standing Firm in the Faith," Ligonier Ministries notes the following:

"Human beings bear a great deal of dignity by virtue of the fact that we are made in God's image (Gen. 1:26–27). Yet the marring of this image in the fall also means that we give ourselves over to many indignities; corruption. One manifestation of this reality is our willingness to abandon truth when the going gets tough or when we simply tire of fighting the spiritual battle. Thus, we find many encouragements in Scripture for the Lord's people to stand firm and not to waffle regarding their reliance upon God for salvation."

"It was for freedom that Christ set us free; therefore keep standing firm and do not be subject again to a yoke of slavery." (Galatians 5:1)

The Galatians 5:1 passage speaks to the fact that we once bore a yoke of slavery both prior to coming to faith in Jesus Christ, as well as the times when we, as Christian men, have stumbled. You know, if we repeat what we've done in the past, the consequences and the outcome never changes. How did that work for you in the past? It's never worked well for me.

All Christian men have known the yoke of slavery. Certainly before coming to Jesus Christ, we wore that yoke as if it was little more than a T-shirt or some other piece of apparel. It came naturally for us to do so. We were spiritually blind at the time.

Yet, all too often those of us in Christ have willingly, or by default, taken that old yoke back upon ourselves. Scripture tells us that that yoke is a yoke of slavery. It's more than just dead weight, it is spiritual darkness.

I heard Dr. Ed Young make this comment on the radio: "It's easier to get a person out of slavery than it is to get slavery out of a person."

But what is it we are called to when we are commanded to act like men?

A True Man Acts like a Man

> *"Be on the alert, stand firm in the faith, **act like men**, be strong" (1 Corinthians 16:13; emphasis mine)*

Let's look at a four specific areas that will best instruct us how to act like men - in our thought life, our words, our deeds, and by our dress (Ephesians 6:10-18).

In Our Thoughts...

> *"Do not conform to the pattern of this world, but be transformed by the renewing of your mind. Then you will be able to test and approve what God's will is—his good, pleasing and perfect will." (Romans 12:2)*

I had to include the Romans 12:2 passage again because years ago someone said to me that I was too intelligent to be a Christian. (Huh!?) On the surface I wasn't sure how to take what she said, but I'll never forget my response. "The Word of God says that I am transformed by the renewal of my mind, not by its removal!"

The renewal of our minds is paramount in the sanctification process of a growing Christian. It's the desired death of garbage in – garbage out.

What is happening on the inside of a Christian man, within our hearts and minds, expresses itself externally. Our thoughts are a driving influence in that they will direct us for good or for ill. Again, for this reason, we must take every thought captive.

> *We are destroying speculations and every lofty thing raised up against the knowledge of God, and we are taking every thought captive to the obedience of Christ, (2 Corinthians 10:5)*

One of the joys I know in Christ is that I can bring everything before Him, all that I am. I can be honest with Him about everything because He already knows it. God knows I still struggle against that old nature. I'm that cowboy on a wildly bucking bronco, and I've been tossed a time or twenty by it.

God knows infinitely more about us than we do about ourselves, about what is in our heart and mind, and He loves us. If you are in Christ, He knows you and your everything, and He loves you. We can come before Him with all that is within us, even when all that is within us is so lacking. In this I speak of me.

Men, we can bring our thoughts before God. We can tell Him about what we thought about and entertained just minutes before we bowed our head in prayer. I have found that when I confess to God the lustful or ungodly thoughts I just had, it is as if that confession grounds the thought and takes away the spark and power from the very thoughts I had or entertained. It neutralizes them.

To confess to God means to agree with Him about our actions; our thoughts, words, or deeds that are out of alignment with His Word. Confessing to God is acting like a man.

God already knows what we need, but like a loving father, He wants us to come to Him and ask.

We can come to God and love Him with all our hearts, minds, and our strength, yet it's discouraging to admit that I have not yet arrived at that point in my day to day walk with Him. Again, truth be told, none of us will until we awake one blessed day in the presence of Jesus Christ. So we must take our thoughts captive to Christ. We must rely upon the Holy Spirit of God to direct us in our thoughts, words, and our deeds.

In Our Words...

The four passages of Scripture below are only four of many that address the words we speak - the heartfelt expressions that our words give voice to.

> *"What goes into someone's mouth does not defile them, but what comes out of their mouth that is what defiles them." (Matthew 15:11)*

> *"He who guards his mouth and his tongue, guards his soul from troubles." (Proverbs 21:23)*

> *"Death and life are in the power of the tongue, and those who love it will eat its fruits." (Proverbs 18:21)*

> *"Therefore consider the members of your earthly body as dead to immorality, impurity, passion, evil desire, and greed, which amounts to idolatry. For it is because of these things that the wrath of God will come upon the sons of disobedience, and in them you also once walked, when you were living in them. But now you also, put them all aside: anger, wrath, malice, slander, and abusive speech from your mouth." (Colossians 3:5-8)*

Each of these four passages speaks of the power of the tongue. Let's take a look at the power of our words.

Our Words Have Power

Whoever said "Sticks and stones will break my bones, but words will never harm me" lied! Words have power. Our words have power. There's something in the Word of God that speaks so clearly on this point, but it is something we can so easily read right past and miss. It is Genesis 1:26-27.

Then God said, "Let Us make man in Our image, according to Our likeness; and let them rule over the fish of the sea and over the birds of the sky and over the cattle and over all the earth, and over every creeping thing that creeps on the earth." God created man in His own image, in the image of God He created him; male and female He created them." (Genesis 1:26-27)

God's spoken Word has power! God spoke all things into being and we are created in His image. In that we are created in His image, our spoken words have power. They have the power to edify, to build up, to encourage, etc. But they can also do harm - to discourage, condemn, and even destroy.

When toxic words come out of us, (I call toxic words 'lava'), they spew out from within us and always initially damage those closest to us. Gossip is lava, slander is lava, ugly words and telling lies, is lava.

Passages That Speak to the Power of our Words

"With it we bless our Lord and Father, and with it we curse men, who have been made in the likeness of God; from the same mouth come both blessing and cursing. My brethren, these things ought not to be this way. Does a fountain send out from the same opening both fresh and bitter water? Can a fig tree, my brethren, produce olives, or a vine produce figs? Nor can salt water produce fresh." (James 3:9-14)

"If anyone thinks himself to be religious, and yet does not bridle his tongue but deceives his own heart, this man's religion is worthless." (James 1:26)

These passages are about maintaining a tight rein on our tongues. Only by the power of the indwelling Holy Spirit are we able to bridle the tongue.

In Our Deeds...

I heard the following comment on the radio by Alistair Begg. His comment sets the table in regards to what we are to be about daily in our lives. He said this: Pleasing God is the foundation for all of our ethical behavior.

In light of this, how are we to act like men, specifically as it concerns the works we do - our deeds?

Let's consider deeds as anything and everything we put our heart, our mind, and our hands to. Good deeds are acts of Christ-centered love expressed towards another. Our good deeds are not to be seen as a basis for our salvation, but rather as an evidence of it.

In our own strength our good deeds, our best efforts, are sin-laden. The good deeds the Word of God speaks of are those deeds that are Spirit-led.

> *"in all things show yourself to be an example of good deeds, with purity in doctrine, dignified, sound in speech which is beyond reproach, so that the opponent will be put to shame, having nothing bad to say about us." (Titus 2:7-8)*

The passage above spells out what it is to act like a man in all we put our hands and hearts to:

- To act like a man, we are to show ourselves to be an example of good deeds.
- Our doctrine must be pure. A man of God knows the Word of God and continues to make a diligent study of it daily.
- A man is to be dignified and under control.
- A man's words are to be truthful and trustworthy.

> *"Let your light so shine before men that they may see your good deeds and give glory to your father in heaven." (Matthew 5:16)*

Our good deeds declare the awesome works of God in our lives. People who have rejected God, or who are spiritually blinded, will push back against us. Tragically, but truthfully, many push back against us because of the poor examples that various people who claim to be Christian have set.

There have been times that someone has spoken just that to me. You know, initially I will agree with them and apologize for what they have experienced before offering this: "Please do not confuse Christianity with Jesus Christ because we, as Christians, all too often do a very poor job of reflecting Him and of being Him to others."

If we are faithful and consistent in how we are daily reliving the life of Jesus Christ, our words and our actions will reflect this to those around us, and to the Lord.

> *"Christ gave himself for us to redeem us from all iniquity and to purify for himself a people of his own who are zealous for good deeds." (Titus 3:14)*

Men, again, we need each other. We are fellow soldiers. Left to our own devices we are inclined to withdraw and keep to ourselves. In such ways, we become MIA's (missing in action) in service to our Lord and to others. By nature, we are inclined to reinhabit the very cave that we once lived in. As a new creation in Jesus Christ, the capacity to both do good deeds and to live in good deeds, already exists within us. The Lord would have us seek His will about where to serve others in His name and to fellowship with our brothers in arms. We must not isolate ourselves.

> *For I am confident of this very thing, that He who began a good work in you will perfect it until the day of Christ Jesus." (Philippians 1:6)*

A True Man is Commanded to be Strong

> *"Be on the alert, stand firm in the faith, act like men, **be strong**" (1 Corinthians 16:13; emphasis mine)*

81

> *"Finally, be strong in the Lord and in the strength of His might." (Ephesians 6:10)*

The beauty of this passage in Ephesians is that we are to be strong in the Lord. What the world considers strength is diametrically opposed to what the Word of God teaches about strength, true strength. Our strength in the Lord has no bearing on our physical strength, or on how often we physically exercise, or how many reps of a given exercise we can muster at a given time.

For a number of years I exercised. Sometimes I even enjoyed it. I've never had a membership at a gym; rather I exercised at home on a weight-lifting devise I purchased years ago. But it seemed no matter how much I exercised, I always found that I measured up short of other men I knew or saw, or of the man I wanted to be. In a true sense, exercise in and of itself became something of an exercise in futility for me.

> **"He gives strength to the weary and increases the power of the weak." (Isaiah. 40:29)**

Our strength comes from God. It's in His strength that we act and in His strength we overcome. The strength I desire to exercise is my strength in Jesus Christ and I am still learning to do so.

> *"I pray that out of his glorious riches he may strengthen you with power through his Spirit in your inner being," (Ephesians 3:16)*

A True Man Witnesses

I've heard it said that you can count the seeds in an apple, but you cannot count the apples in a seed. This speaks to the fact that we cannot truly know what may become of the times we witness and share our faith with non-believers. We are commanded to sow righteousness.

> *"For the report of your obedience has reached to all; therefore I am rejoicing over you, but I want you to be wise in what is good, and innocent in what is evil." (Romans 16:19)*

To be innocent of evil is to recognize what evil is and choose to look the other direction. That's at the heart of repentance. It's a Spirit-led about face. A true man shares with others about the about-face in his own life, that the power of God might be displayed in him.

Again, not only are we to be witnesses, we're to be evidence of a changed life and share about it. We are to be a reflection of Jesus Christ.

"Do they see Jesus in me?"

There's a wonderful passage in the book of Malachi that states this about the words we speak of God and of Jesus Christ - about when we witness of Him:

> *"Then those who feared the LORD spoke to one another, and the LORD gave attention and heard it, and a book of remembrance was written before Him for those who fear the LORD and who esteem His name." (Malachi 3:16)*

Scripture is clear that loyalty to God does not go unnoticed or unrewarded. Certainly, God does not need a written record in order to keep track of human deeds. However, when He speaks to us, He often uses metaphor or parable to help us understand. God makes it clear that He hears and knows the intent of every heart and desires to honor those who honor Him.

A True Man Dresses for Success

Likely you've heard the expression "Dress for Success." Given the battleground we find ourselves daily enmeshed in, there is no greater dress for success than is found in Ephesians 6:10-18.

My brothers, the below passages in Ephesians chapter 6 specifically instructs us on how best to stand against the enemy of our souls. If we miss or ignore any of these verses, we do so at our own peril. In Ephesians 6:10-17, each piece of armor is a quality, not a function.

> *"Finally, be strong in the Lord and in the strength of His might. Put on the full armor of God, so that you will be able to stand firm against the schemes of the devil. For our struggle is not against flesh and blood, but against the rulers, against the powers, against the world forces of this darkness, against the spiritual forces of wickedness in the heavenly places. (Ephesians 6:10-12)*

> *Therefore, take up the full armor of God, so that you will be able to resist in the evil day, and having done everything, to stand firm. Stand firm therefore, having girded your loins with truth, and having put on the breastplate of righteousness, and having shod your feet with the preparation of the gospel of peace; in addition to all, taking up the shield of faith with which you will be able to extinguish all the flaming arrows of the evil one. And take the helmet of salvation, and the sword of the Spirit, which is the word of God. With all prayer and petition pray at all times in the Spirit, and with this in view, be on the alert with all perseverance and petition for all the saints," (Ephesians 6:13-18)*

Although the spiritual armor pieces spoken of in these passages are invisible to the human eye, they are Godly qualities and adorning ourselves spiritually in each one is essential in our daily walk with Jesus Christ to protect us against the continual onslaught by the enemy of our souls. At its essence, what we are putting on in each case is Jesus Christ Himself.

There are a great number of books and Christian internet sites that have far more excellent material on this subject, but for my purposes here I'll briefly reference and speak to each of the six spiritual pieces of apparel we are to adorn ourselves with.

The Belt of Truth… (Ephesians 6:14a)

The belt of truth holds together all we are to spiritually adorn ourselves with. In my mind's eye, I see it as the belt that is awarded to a prize fighter after he wins the boxing match against his number-one ranked opponent. In the day of the Romans, the belt around them held up their cloak or the coat they wore so that it would not encumber them as they ran forward into battle. Every piece of the full armor depends upon the belt of truth.

Truth holds everything together!

The Breastplate of Righteousness… (Ephesians 6:14b)

The breastplate of righteousness is the spiritual adornment that guards our heart. The heart is the most vulnerable part of any Christian man - it's what the enemy wants to assault and recapture. The righteousness referenced in the name of this piece of spiritual armor is the righteousness of our Lord and Savior Jesus Christ. The breastplate the Roman soldiers Paul observed covered both their front and their back.

Feet Shod with the Preparation of the Gospel of Peace… (Ephesians 6:15)

Our feet represent our wills - our feet take us where we want to go. God's peace is our compass. His peace gives us balance, puts our priorities in order, and helps us follow His will. When our feet are shod with the gospel of peace, we will only go where God's peace leads us to go. The kind of Christian soldier who will be victorious on the battlefield is the one who is balanced, who has good mobility, and who uses every opportunity to stand firm and to share the gospel.

The gospel of peace is a peace that comes to us in and through the Word of God and makes us immovable in battle. We are to take with us the gospel of Jesus Christ everywhere we go. There is a wonderful "stand firm" element here.

In the days of the Roman legions (which, no doubt, Paul made a close study of), soldiers' sandals often had metal spikes (hobnails) woven into them that protruded from the bottom making it more difficult for an enemy to push them back as they attacked. This way they were able to hold the ground on which they stood. Men, we are to stand firm, even if we must stand alone. We stand firm on the Word of God as we take it everywhere we go.

> *"Now, brothers, I want to remind you of the gospel I preached to you, which you received, and in which you stand firm." (1 Corinthians 15:1)*

The assault against us comes from every side, but we are to hold our ground in Jesus Christ. We don't battle to win this war – it has already been won by the shed blood of Jesus Christ, the Son of God and by His blood shed on our behalf. Satan is simply walking the green mile, heading towards his inevitable end in hell. His sentence has been cast, but his execution has yet to be carried out.

We'll be dressed in white when this happens. I once thought this odd, to be dressed in white for battle?! Yes, because Satan's execution will be carried out by the spoken word of the Living Word, Jesus Christ. How awesome that moment will be.

The Shield of Faith… (Ephesians 6:16)

This is a spiritually powerful defensive weapon against all that Satan attacks us with. Faith in God is what this powerful spiritual shield represents. All too often during times of hardship and other great challenges in our lives, we can easily begin to allow doubt to creep into our minds and spirit. We can begin to doubt God and we can begin to doubt the truth and veracity of His Word. This spiritual shield, the Shield of Faith, protects us when we are under attack, but only if it is in our spiritual possession.

> *"Every word of God is tested; He is a shield to those who take refuge in Him." (Proverbs 30:5)*

The Helmet of Salvation… (Ephesians 6:17a)

> *"For who has known the mind of the Lord, that he will instruct Him? But we have the mind of Christ." (1 Corinthians 2:16)*

The Helmet of Salvation guards our head and, thus, our mind. Our mind is our storehouse of knowledge and of all the memories of all we have experienced. Satan wants to pollute our minds. He wants to resurrect our old ways of thinking and behaving. He wants to rekindle what once burned so within us; those old ways of living and reacting to the world around us and the thought life from within us.

> *"Therefore if anyone is in Christ, he is a new creation; the old things passed away; behold, new things have come." (2 Corinthians 5:17)*

In my life I have even found the comfort and need to wear it myself as I lay my head down on my pillow to sleep.

The Sword of the Spirit... (Ephesians 6:17b)

No doubt, if you've ever done a study of the Full Armor of God you've heard that the Sword of the Spirit is the only offensive weapon of the six referenced. This sword is the offensive weapon Jesus used against Satan when He was tempted while in the wilderness.

The Word of God is our number one defense against Satan. We assault him with it when we speak it. He is a defeated foe, condemned forever by the substitutional and sacrificial shed blood of Jesus Christ, our Savior and Lord - Hallelujah!

> *Therefore, my beloved brethren whom I long to see, my joy and crown, in this way stand firm in the Lord, my beloved. (Philippians 4:1)*

Strength is revealed and increased through our exercise of faith and thru the Word of God and by the indwelling Spirit of God.

> *"Be strong and courageous, for you shall give this people possession of the land which I swore to their fathers to give them. Only be strong and very courageous; be careful to do according to all the law which Moses My servant commanded*

> *you; do not turn from it to the right or to the left, so that you may have success wherever you go." Have I not commanded you? Be strong and courageous! Do not tremble or be dismayed, for the Lord your God is with you wherever you go." (Joshua 1:6-7 & 9)*

> *"It was for freedom that Christ set us free; therefore keep standing firm and do not be subject again to a yoke of slavery." (Galatians 5:1)*

A True Man Loves

True men love God and love others. Jesus Christ embodies this.

> *"A new commandment I give to you, that you love one another, even as I have loved you, that you also love one another. By this all men will know that you are My disciples, if you have love for one another." (John 13:34-35)*

> ### *Jesus Christ is our greatest example of love.*

> *"For God so loved the world, that He gave His only begotten Son, that whoever believes in Him shall not perish, but have eternal life. (John 3:16)*

The phrase 'only begotten' means unique - the only one of His kind - that is who Jesus is.

Jesus loved us sacrificially (2 Corinthians 5:21) and unconditionally (Romans 5:8). We are to love others in the same way Jesus loves us.

> *He made Him who knew no sin to be sin on our behalf, so that we might become the righteousness of God in Him. (2 Corinthians 5:21)*

> *But God demonstrates His own love toward us, in that while we were yet sinners, Christ died for us. Romans 5:8)*

A True Man Loves His Wife...

> *"Husbands, love your wives, just as Christ also loved the church and gave Himself up for her," (Ephesians 5:25)*

In an excellent online article about the love a Christian man should exhibit towards his wife, I found the following written on May 22, 2013 by a blogger for Ligonier Ministries named William Boekestein titled "Husbands, 8 Admonitions to Love Your Wife." I provide below only summary points from his excellent and insightful blog.

When God says, "Husbands, love your wives," he speaks of the woman as a complex being. He calls every man to love his whole wife just as every man loves his whole self (Ephesians 5:29). This means that a husband must do all he can to understand his wife's world. What follows are eight admonitions to love our wives with respect to their various facets.

A husband is to love his wife's:

- Heart - Emotional Love
- Mind - Intellectual Love
- Body - Physical Love
- Soul - Spiritual Love
- Relationships - Relational Love
- Humanity – Realistic love (that she, as you, will make mistakes)
- Calling - Supportive Love
- Maker - Theological Love

Ultimately, we are loveless because we love ourselves more than we love God and are dissatisfied with God's provision. This means that the more you love God the better equipped you will be to truly love your wife.

> *But not one has done so who has a remnant of the Spirit. And what did that one do while he was seeking a godly offspring?*

> *Take heed then to your spirit, and let no one deal treacherously against the wife of your youth. For I hate divorce," says the* LORD, *the God of Israel, "and him who covers his garment with wrong," says the* LORD *of hosts. "So take heed to your spirit, that you do not deal treacherously." (Malachi 2:15-16)*

In her book, *'The Dating Manifesto,' (David C. Cook, 2015)*, author Lisa Anderson insightfully notes:

"Yes, the Bible begins with marriage. But
it also ends with marriage."

God is, indeed, preparing a bride (the church) for His Son, His only begotten Son.

A True Man Loves His Children…

I offer the below few bullet points that I trust will capture the heart of what the Word of God says about loving our children.

- Show your son how to be a strong, courageous, and compassionate Godly young man. Tell him you love him. Demonstrate it by your words and deeds. Show him how a man loves his wife by the loving and gracious way you treat your wife, his mother.
- Show your daughter how a man is to love a woman - the regard and respect she should expect. Demonstrate it by the way you treat your wife, her mother, by encouraging her. Tell her that you love her.
- Show your children daily, by your actions, what the love of a Godly father looks like.
- Show them the love our heavenly Father has for us. Point them to Him - point them to Jesus!

> *"Behold, children are a gift of the* LORD, *the fruit of the womb is a reward. Like arrows in the hand of a warrior, so are the children of one's youth. How blessed is the man whose*

quiver is full of them; they will not be ashamed when they speak with their enemies in the gate." (Psalm 127: 3-5)

I enjoy keeping a small ziplock baggie of nice manufactured stone arrowheads in my backpack and am often led to give one to the parents of young children I see when I am out and about. I always reference Psalm 127:3-5, noting the below:

Arrows aren't to remain in the quiver. They are to be focused AND released!

A True Man Loves God...

"Teacher, which is the great commandment in the Law?" And He said to him, "'You shall love the Lord your God with all your heart, and with all your soul, and with all your mind.' This is the great and foremost commandment. The second is like it, 'You shall love your neighbor as yourself.' On these two commandments depend the whole Law and the Prophets." (Matthew 22:36-40)

That first command is a tough one to live out. Sure, we can say we love God in such a way, but does our day to day life reflect this. Ask God to reveal your heart to you in this regard. He greatly desires such love and wouldn't include a command that we can't or couldn't follow.

This second command refers to our love for all mankind, again, the good, the bad, and the ugly (I like that expression). We have all known such ones in our lives. Likely, we each have been all three at one time or another. We as Christians are to be identified by our love for others and by our love for one another.

A new commandment I give to you, that you love one another, even as I have loved you, that you also love one another. (John 13:34)

This command given by Jesus refers to our love for fellow believers and those that do not yet know Him. True followers of Jesus Christ are identified by their love for one another.

A True Man Worships...

> *"But an hour is coming, and now is, when the true worshipers will worship the Father in spirit and truth; for such people the Father seeks to be His worshipers. God is spirit, and those who worship Him must worship in spirit and truth."* (John 4:23-24)

My brothers, a great number of excellent books have been written on the subject of worship and, once again, I'll not attempt any such here (sounds like a skipping record, huh?). We are all engaged in war with an invisible but all-surrounding enemy. In this ongoing conflict, worship of God, our Great Commander, is a must.

I want to look at worship thru the eyes of the ninth chapter of the gospel of John. The entire ninth chapter of the book of John is about Jesus' healing of the man born blind. This chapter is rich with insight, intrigue, and truth. The miracle of the healing of the man born blind is clearly a parable in action. We must embrace it as such so as to get at the deeper meaning of it.

> *"As He passed by, He saw a man blind from birth. And His disciples asked Him, "Rabbi, who sinned, this man or his parents, that he would be born blind?"* (John 9:1-2)

Please note two things in this first verse that could easily miss our notice. First, throughout the Scripture, Jesus never just happens to just pass by. This is divine appointment, not happenstance that brings Jesus to this man.

Second, verse 1 says He saw a man born blind from birth. Jesus knew this man was born blind. Truly, the point being is that we are ALL born blind - blinded by sin. It's rather odd to consider that as a newborn child we 'open our eyes' to darkness.

The question put to Jesus by the disciples concerning the man's blindness helps us face the question that all of us have asked or been asked about. Why does God permit suffering to occur? Why would a God of love allow serious ailments and disability to children, or permit horrible accidents to otherwise healthy people. What about war, famine, and disease?

The disciples had evidently been taught, through their upbringing in Judaism, that sin and injury, or handicap, are linked - that human suffering is the result of human sin. Interestingly, Jesus does not deny that. However, He elevates this encounter so as to make it representative to the reader that this man born blind represents each of us - all of humanity. We are all born blind; spiritually blind.

The hardships we experience in this life are not a disaster but an opportunity for certain things to be manifested in our lives, and in the lives of people who come in contact with us. As an example, I have found that others are more open to my witness of Jesus Christ while I'm in my wheelchair than I ever experienced standing erect.

> *Jesus answered, "It was neither that this man sinned, nor his parents;* **but it was so that the works of God might be displayed in him.** *⁴ We must work the works of Him who sent Me as long as it is day; night is coming when no one can work. (John 9:3-4; emphasis mine)*

That the works of God might be displayed through him - I believe that this is what God wants in every believer that comes to faith in Jesus Christ - that the works of God might be displayed in us. We must be about the very things Jesus Christ was about. We are to speak of the Kingdom of God and invite others into it, through Jesus Christ only (John 14:6), while we have life and breath. There is a time coming in each of our lives when this can no longer happen.

> *Jesus said to him, "I am the way, and the truth, and the life; no one comes to the Father but through Me. (John 14:6)*

The works of God are to be displayed in us.

*"While I am in the world, I am the Light of the world."
When He had said this, He spat on the ground, and made
clay of the spittle, and applied the clay to his eyes, (John
9:5-6)*

Again, the man born blind represents all of humanity - born spiritually
blind and spiritually dead.

Do not miss that Jesus spat upon the ground. In Genesis 2:7 we are told
that God formed man from the dust of the ground, from the clay of the
earth. That symbolism is used many times in Scripture. God is the Potter
(Jer. 18:4-6), we are the clay. He molds us and shapes us into what he wants
us to be. Thus, we must allow ourselves to be broken, reshaped, so as to be
better fitted for God's purpose.

Clay pots are not very strong. Clay is not a very powerful substance. It is
malleable and weak. Thus, all through Scripture, clay is used as a symbol
of the weakness and fragility of human nature, and of mankind. We are
all made of clay. We are clay pots. This is what clay symbolizes.

This thought has struck me before - that God spoke all things into being,
but it wasn't until He created man that He got His hands dirty. I believe
there is an intentional relationship between the Genesis 2:9 account and
Jesus' spitting upon the ground and His handling of the clay in John 9:6.

*We are but clay in the hands of a loving and mighty God. Allow
Him to do what pleases Him, that we might please Him.*

*and said to him, "Go, wash in the pool of Siloam" (which is
translated, Sent). So he went away and washed, and came
back seeing. (John 9:7)*

Our walk by faith is much akin to what this man experienced. Christ said
"Go…" and he did. Regardless of the obstacles ahead of him or how he
might be perceived, he was obedient - he went as directed.

Again, the account of the healing of the man born blind is as if a parable. There is a much deeper meaning and truth to it than just a cursory reading might offer. In looking ahead in John 9, we'll see that now our eyes (and his) have been opened physically and spiritually, there is ahead for us, as there was for this man, difficulty.

When Jesus sends this man on a stumbling journey to the pool of Siloam with clay on his eyes, He is indicating that there is a difficult time ahead of him. People will see him as odd or peculiar as he stumbles his way to the pool. The process of healing his physical and spiritual sight will involve a prolonged and difficult journey that will likely be filled with obstacles.

> ### *The world is our battleground. The Word of God is our marching orders in this ongoing conflict.*

> *"These things I have spoken to you, so that in Me you may have peace. In the world you have tribulation, but take courage; I have overcome the world." (John 16:33)*

John 9:8-34 is all about the great controversy about this man now seeing and those present and fully aware of the miracle trying to make sense of it. The Pharisees question and debate the man. The Pharisees make verbal assaults upon Jesus because this healing happened on the Sabbath as the healed man is questioned yet again - even his parents are questioned and, because of their fear of being cast out of the temple, they wimped out. Matter of fact, his parents gave ZERO praise to God for this miracle - that their very own son has been healed. They remained silent before the Pharisees and the Lord.

The parents toss the ball back to the Pharisees and they, once again, question the now-seeing man. He wonderfully answered them about who Jesus is and said this: *"Whether He is a sinner, I do not know; one thing I do know, that though I was blind, now I see." (John 9:25)*

There is salt in this man's words. "Yes, I was born blind, but now I see!"

Salt adds flavor to both food and to words spoken. It preserves what it is applied to, and it cleanses - but it also irritates. The world, the flesh, and the devil are irritated by the Word of God.

> *Jesus heard that they had put him out, & finding him, He said, "Do you believe in the Son of Man?" He answered, "Who is He, Lord that I may believe in Him?" Jesus said to him, "You have both seen Him & He is the one who is talking with you." And he said, "Lord, I believe."* **And he worshiped Him (emphasis mine)**. *(John 9:35-38)*

The words of the man born blind but now seeing irritated the religious rulers. The John 9:8-34 passages are a part of the difficulties and challenges before this man and us. Our eyes have been spiritually opened - we're no longer spiritually dead - how can we not but sing His praises! Verse 38 is where I'm hanging my hat: *And he said, "Lord, I believe." And he worshiped Him. (John 9:38)*

What a beautiful scene. Notice that he did not have to find Jesus. When, in the temporary darkness of his human clay, he was at last brought to recognize who Jesus was, then immediately Jesus found him. Jesus opened his spiritual eyes with the simple words, *"You are looking at him, he who speaks to you is he."* Immediately the man responded by falling on his knees to worship Him - his and our Savior.

What might his worship have looked like? I ask this of each of us. Really, allow your imagination free rein. How do you see this man, who is now physically and spiritually healed and now believing in Jesus, worshipping Him?

That question brings this memory to my mind. I will never forget the day my parents drove me home from a visit with an eye doctor. I was in 7th grade at the time. I had been having headaches in school, only to learn that they came from my having to squint to read the chalkboard because my left eye had been injured in a sporting event.

Well, that afternoon, as I sat in the backseat of my dad's car, my mom handed back to me the glasses I had been prescribed - my first pair ever. The second I put them on it was incredible! It was as if the lights had been turned on around me. It was as if I experienced true three-dimensional sight for the first time. I had never seen the detail of the branches of a tree and the sky and the clouds had color and depth to them. It was as if the Christmas tree I had enjoyed all my life was suddenly lit. I see the healed man born blind in this manner.

It was much this way and more the moment I stood from my knees the night I totally committed my heart and life to Jesus Christ; the night I fully surrendered. I could not but declare His name and give praise to Jesus Christ, and to God my Father. **I worshipped Him that evening!**

Are we blind to what true worship is - to what it might look like - inside and out? I pray not.

> *"Oh give thanks to the Lord, call upon His name; make known His deeds among the peoples. Sing to Him, sing praises to Him; speak of all His wonders. Glory in His holy name; let the heart of those who seek the Lord be glad. Seek the Lord and His strength; seek His face continually." (Psalm 105:1-4)*

Dr. Delesslyn A. Kennebrew offers the following comments about what true worship is.

"There are numerous definitions of the word worship. Yet, one in particular encapsulates the priority we should give to worship as a spiritual discipline: Worship is to honor with extravagant love and extreme submission.... True worship, in other words, is defined by the priority we place on who God is in our lives and where God is on our list of priorities. True worship is a matter of the heart expressed through a lifestyle of holiness. We worship God because he is God. Period."

After reading her comments, I thought of the sticky note that I keep in one of my Bible's that says this:

> **To adore is to recognize the whole of the object of adoration and the nothingness of the adorer.**

A True Man Prays...

In my Christian life I've been blessed to have heard the Full Armor of God taught a number of times by different teachers, but I have been surprised and disappointed a time or two when verse 18 was either minimized or not mentioned.

> *With all prayer and petition pray at all times in the Spirit, and with this in view, be on the alert with all perseverance and petition for all the saints, (Ephesians 6:18)*

The Ephesians 6:10-18 passage is about the ongoing spiritual warfare in our lives. What kind of soldier would we be in this spiritual battle for the souls of people if we had little or no daily contact with God, our great Commander in Chief?

> **"The man who would know God must give time to Him." – A.W. Tozer**

Men, we are to pray. Here are just three suggestions on how to pray.

1) Pray in the Spirit

> *"In the same way the Spirit also helps our weakness; for we do not know how to pray as we should, but the Spirit Himself intercedes for us with groaning's too deep for words; 27 and He who searches the hearts knows what the mind of the Spirit is, because He intercedes for the saints according to the will of God. (Romans 8:26-27)*

GotQuestions.org offers the following on praying in the Spirit: *"The Greek word translated "pray in" can have several different meanings. It can mean "by means of," "with the help of," "in the sphere of," and "in connection to." Praying in the Spirit does not refer to the words we are saying. Rather, it refers to how we are praying. Praying in the Spirit is praying according to the Spirit's leading. It is praying for things the Spirit leads us to pray for."*

2) Pray always

> *"Pray without ceasing; in everything give thanks; for this is God's will for you in Christ Jesus." (1 Thessalonians 5:17-18)*

This passage says to me that we are to live in a spirit of prayer - ever aware of the glory and goodness of God in our lives. We are to be regular and consistent in the exercise of prayer. I have found this happening within me simply when I am driving — even thankful for the light being green, thankful for the gas in my truck tank, etc.

3) Pray and Be Alert

> *"Keep watching and praying that you may not come into temptation; the spirit is willing, but the flesh is weak." Mark 14:38)*

Again, Proverbs 7 speaks of our natural inclination and ability to rationalize our 'further investigation' (our giving ourselves permission to pursue) that which is calling out to us. We, in effect, construct rational lies about our draw into sin.

> *"He who separates himself seeks his own desire, he quarrels against all sound wisdom." (Proverbs 18:1)*

Years ago, after having finished reading A. W. Tozer's, *'The Pursuit of God,'* I noted that there were several personally impacting truths that confronted me. First and foremost was this - I wish I could sellout totally to Jesus Christ. This remains to this day a particular source of frustration to me.

I cannot simply recognize that I need to move in that direction, only to do little about it.

God sees the big picture - we see mere shadows at best. But I have come to realize that not tomorrow, or next week, or next month will I become completely sold-out to Him, though that is what I want. It, the selling out process is a part of the transformation process that is ongoing in our lives.

We must recognize this as God's goal for us and we must yield our wills and our desires to Him. The world has been too much within us – within me.

> *"Do you not know? Have you not heard? The Everlasting God, the LORD, the Creator of the ends of the earth does not become weary or tired. His understanding is inscrutable. He gives strength to the weary, and to him who lacks might He increases power. Though youths grow weary and tired, and vigorous young men stumble badly, yet those who wait for the LORD will gain new strength; they will mount up with wings like eagles, they will run and not get tired, they will walk and not become weary." (Isaiah 40:28-31)*

Act like a Man - a Godly Man!

Study Guide - Chapter 4

Day 1

a) How would you honestly describe your prayer life?
b) What might be lacking?

Responses:

Reflect upon the following passage: *"Be of sober spirit, be on the alert. Your adversary, the devil, prowls around like a roaring lion, seeking someone to devour." (1 Peter 5:8)*

c) In your life, have you ever heard the roar of Satan, or has he attempted to operate more silently in your life - as if behind the scenes?

d) Describe your response? Make mention of the enemy's 'behind the scenes' assaults you've experienced.

Responses:

Day 2

Passage: *"Be on the alert, stand firm in the faith, act like men, be strong" (1 Corinthians 16:13)*

a) Regarding the command that we are to stand firm, what are some of the areas that you have discerned about the schemes (manners) of Satan's attacks that have the ability to thwart your ability, from time to time, to stand firm?

b) What have you seen around you in regards to how unsaved men behave? What does it seem to you that they 'stand' for?

Responses:

c) Regarding the statement made earlier in this chapter – 'Confession to God is acting like a man,' – consider and describe how you have confessed to God things regarding your thought life?

d) What areas in your thought life do you need to most keep on the alert about?

Responses:

Day 3

Passage: *"What goes into someone's mouth does not defile them, but what comes out of their mouth that is what defiles them." (Matthew 15:11)*

a) Given that words have power, what words have been spoken to you in the past that, to this day, you can still hear? Maybe they were good words, maybe not.
b) Do those words somehow define you in some way today?
c) Do they sometimes play in your mind?

Responses:

Day 4

Passage: *"Be on the alert, stand firm in the faith, act like men,* **be strong***" (1 Corinthians 16:13)*

a) How do you define manly strength?
b) Consider your response to the above and then define 'godly strength.'

Responses:

Day 5

Read and reflect upon the following passages. How do they speak to you as being a man, a Godly man?

Passage: *"The Sovereign LORD is my strength; he makes my feet like the feet of a deer, he enables me to tread on the heights." (Habakkuk 3:19)*

Response:

Passage: *"Have I not commanded you? Be strong and courageous! Do not tremble or be dismayed, for the LORD your God is with you wherever you go." (Joshua 1:9)*

Response:

Passage: *"But he said to me, "My grace is sufficient for you, for my power is made perfect in weakness." Therefore I will boast all the more gladly about my weaknesses, so that Christ's power may rest on me. That is why, for Christ's sake, I delight in weaknesses, in insults, in hardships, in persecutions, in difficulties. For when I am weak, then I am strong." (2 Corinthians 12:9-10)*

Response:

Passage: *"The LORD is my strength and my defense; he has become my salvation." (Psalm 118:14)*

Response:

Passage: *"He gives strength to the weary and increases the power of the weak. Even youths grow tired and weary, and young men stumble and fall; but those who hope in the LORD will renew their strength. They will soar on wings like eagles; they will run and not grow weary, they will walk and not be faint." (Isaiah 40:29-31)*

Response:

Passage: *"Love the Lord your God with all your heart and with all your soul and with all your mind and with all your strength." (Mark 12:30)*

Response:

Chapter 5
WHEN GOD SPEAKS

"I have told you these things, so that in me you may have peace. In this world you will have trouble. But take heart! I have overcome the world." (John 16:33)

<u>God, our Supreme Commander</u>

God is our Supreme High Commander. When He speaks, we are to listen and obey. Refresh your warrior-self in the following passage (Psalm 44:4-8):

> *"You are my King, O God; command victories for Jacob. Through You we will push back our adversaries; through Your name we will trample down those who rise up against us. For I will not trust in my bow, nor will my sword to save me. But You have saved us from our adversaries, and You have put to shame those who hate us. In God we have boasted all day long, and we will give thanks to Your name forever. Selah" (Psalm 44:4-8)*

Before continuing, I want to speak for a moment on the word Selah. Amongst the number of ways this word has been translated include: to pause, crescendo, musical interlude, praise, and lift up.

Got Questions.org defines Selah this way:

"When we see the word selah in a psalm or in Habakkuk 3, we should pause to carefully weigh the meaning of what we have just read or heard, lifting up our hearts in praise to God for His great truths."

I personally have taken Selah as being <u>a pregnant pause</u>, meaning that I am to stop and reflect on what I just read. I believe I am to focus and meditate on what I just read and in doing so, the Holy Spirit might <u>give birth</u> to my mind and heart to what the Lord is saying to me in a given Psalm. For that matter, we should do the same after reading any part of the Bible, not just a given Psalm. I have been blessed by doing so on many occasions.

I once heard the dear saint, J. Vernon McGee, define Selah as meaning "Stop, look, and listen." I like that. It was a part of my high school football fight song.

When our Supreme Commander speaks, we must listen. We must take to heart His commands and directives. We are to read and reflect upon what the Word of God says to us. We must invite the Holy Spirit to open our minds and hearts to the Bible. We are to ask the Lord for wisdom - James 1:5-6.

> *But if any of you lacks wisdom, let him ask of God, who gives to all generously and without reproach, and it will be given to him. But he must ask in faith without any doubting, for the one who doubts is like the surf of the sea, driven and tossed by the wind. (James 1:5-6)*

God knows everything from eternity past to eternity future, and He is intimately familiar with the world we live in, the enemy we war against, and with us. Nothing escapes Him.

As I was reading the book of Jeremiah, I noticed the repeated use of the phrase "The Lord of Heaven's armies says," or words to this effect. The New American Standard uses the words, "the Lord of hosts." The word hosts is interchangeable with heaven's armies, as is used in the New Living Translation.

I highlighted the phrase when used in the book of Jeremiah as I found them in my reading. I counted it used 83 times. I state this to simply reinforce the fact that God is our High Commander. He is the God of Heaven's armies, both in heaven and on earth.

Next, let's take a look at some of the many qualities of God - qualities that should make certain to us that He and He alone is God, and that we can trust Him fully and completely in all things – and certainly in the battle we are engaged in as Christian men. This will help grow our understanding about how mighty our Great Supreme Commander is.

Qualities of God

I am grateful to Josh McDowell ministries for their permission to include the following qualities of Almighty God. This tremendous resource will help us to better discover and greater appreciate the awesome Holy God we serve.

At the time of this writing, this must visit site is: https://www.josh.org/resources/spiritual-growth/attributes-of-god/

Because God is all-powerful, He can help me with anything.

- God has the power to create anything from nothing (Ps. 33:6-9)
- God has power to deliver (Exod. 13:3)
- God's creative power is beyond our comprehension (Job 38:1-11)
- God speaks and things happen (Ps. 29:3-9)
- His resurrection power is immeasurably great (Eph. 1:19-20)
- His creation reflects His power (Ps. 19:1-4)
- His powerful word sustains everything (Heb. 1:3)
- He has power over death (Rev. 1:18)
- No one can challenge what God does (Dan. 4:35)
- Reveals Himself as the almighty God (Gen. 17:1)

Because God is ever-present, He is always with me.

- all creation is dependent upon His presence (Col. 1:17)
- God's continual presence brings contentment (Heb. 13:5)
- God is everywhere and no one can escape Him (Ps. 139:7-12)
- no task is too large or too difficult for Him (Jer. 32:17, 27)
- One cannot hide from God (Jer. 23:23-24)

Because God is sovereign, I will joyfully submit to His will.

- God controls time and seasons (Dan. 2:21)
- God powerfully delivered His people from Egypt (Exod. 12:29-32; 13:13-31)
- God has dominion over the affairs of people (Job 12:13-25)
- God controls nature for His purposes (Job 37:2-13)
- God chose His people to become like Christ (Rom. 8:28-30)
- God chose His people before He made the world (Eph. 1:4)
- God's eternal purpose is to make His wisdom known (Eph. 3:10-11)
- He raises and removes rulers (Dan. 2:21)
- He has a plan for His people and will carry it out (Eph. 1:5, 11)
- He chose His people to save and purify them (2 Thess. 2:13)
- He is the only Sovereign (1 Tim. 1:17; 6:15)
- The Creator looks after His creation (Ps. 104:3-32)
- The powerful Creator reduces human rulers to nothing (Isa. 40:21-26)
- Relationship with God requires worship (John 4:24)
- God has dominion over the affairs of people (Job 12.13-25)
- God controls nature for His purposes (Job 37:2-13)
- God chose His people to become like Christ (Rom. 8:28-30)
- God chose His people before He made the world (Eph. 1:4)
- God's eternal purpose is to make His wisdom known (Eph. 3:10-11)
- He raises and removes rulers (Dan. 2:21)
- He has a plan for His people and will carry it out (Eph. 1:5, 11)

- He chose His people to save and purify them (2 Thess. 2:13)
- He is the only Sovereign (1 Tim. 1:17; 6:15)

Because God is holy, I will devote myself to Him in purity, worship, and service.

- God guards His holy reputation (Ezek. 36:21-23)
- God's holiness demands exclusive worship (Josh. 24:19)
- He disciplines believers to impart His holiness to them (Heb. 12:10)
- His holiness is unique (Exod. 15:11)
- His holiness is the standard for believers' behavior (Lev. 19:2; 1 Pet. 1:15-16)
- His holy presence rejects impurity (Isa. 6:3-5)
- No one else is holy like He is (1 Sam. 2:2)
- The most holy One deserves constant honor (Rev. 4:8)

Because God is absolute truth, I will believe what He says and live accordingly.

- believers know that God is true (John 3:33)
- eternal life is knowing the only true God (John 17:3)
- even if all humanity lies, God remains true (Rom. 3:4)
- God is the Truth (John 14:6)
- God follows through on His promises (Num. 11:22-23; 31-34)
- God's words are true and completely righteous (Ps. 19:9)
- God's truth is everlasting (Ps. 117:2)
- God's word is truth (John 17:17)
- God's words are faithful and true (Rev. 21:5; 22:6)
- God's truth can be suppressed to our peril (Rom. 1: 1 8ff)
- He is "the God of truth" (Ps. 31:5; Isa. 65:16)
- God doesn't lie but keeps His word (Num. 23:19)
- He is full of grace and truth (John 1:14)
- His Spirit guides believers into all truth (John 16:13)

- the Holy Spirit is characterized by truth in every way (John 14:17; 15:26; 1 John 5:6)
- true freedom comes from abiding in God's truth (John 8:31-32)

Because God is righteous, I will live by His standards.

- His righteousness is absolute (Ps. 71:19)
- He rules out of righteousness (Ps. 97:2)
- He is righteous in everything He does (Ps. 145:17)
- He delights in demonstrating righteousness (Jer. 9:24)
- in the end, the righteous Judge will judge righteously (2 Tim. 4:8)
- people must declare humbly God alone is righteous (Exod. 9:27; 2 Chron. 12:6)
- the Lord's name: "The Lord is our righteousness" (Jer. 23:6; 33:16)

Because God is just, He will always treat me fairly.

- a day is fixed for His righteous judgment of the world (Acts 17:31)
- all sin is ultimately against a righteous God (Ps. 51:4)
- all God's ways are righteous and deserve praise (Rev. 15:3)
- God alone is the judge (James 4:12)
- God judges all people with justice (Ps. 9:7-8)
- God's law and judgments are completely righteous (Ps. 19:7-9)
- He exercises justice toward all humanity (Gen. 18:25)
- He is just in all His ways (Dent. 32:4)
- God rightly judges heart, mind and deeds (Jer. 17:10)
- Jesus, our righteous defender before the Father (1 John 2:1)
- the Messiah will judge all with complete justice (Isa. 11:4-5)
- the righteous Messiah will establish a righteous people (Jer. 33:16)
- the righteous God justifies those who believe in Jesus (Rom. 3:25-26)

Because God is love, He is unconditionally committed to my well-being.

- as a father, God corrects His beloved children (Prov. 3:12)
- believers should imitate God's universal love (Matt. 5:44-45)

- eternal plans are motivated by His love (Eph. 1:4-5)
- God loves and preserves His godly people (Ps. 37:28)
- God loves His people, even when they are faithless (Hos. 3:1)
- God deserves thanks because of His perpetual love (Ps. 100:5)
- God loved the world enough to send His Son to die (John 3:16)
- God loves those who love His Son (and obey Him) (John 14:21)
- His love is poured into believers' hearts (Rom. 5:5)
- God is love, and those who know God love others (I John 4:7-8, 20-21)
- nothing can separate the believer from His love (Rom. 8:38-39)
- to love enemies and the wicked is to be like God (Luke 6:35)

Because God is merciful, He forgives me of my sins when I sincerely confess them.

- God will never relent from showing mercy to His children (Ps. 23:6)
- God will listen to our pleas for mercy (Ps. 30:8)
- Because of mercy, God washes away our transgressions (Ps. 51:1)
- Because God is merciful, He has not hidden Himself from us (Ps. 69:16)
- Mercy comes to those who confess their sins (Prov. 28:13)
- Mercy is given to those who are themselves merciful (Matt. 5:7)
- God desires to show mercy to His people instead of having His people trying to obtain their own righteousness (Matt. 9:13)
- God shows mercy to those who fear His name (Luke 1:50)
- Our mercy of others should be an imitation of God's mercy to us (Luke 6:36)
- Knowing God's mercy encourages us to follow Him (Rom. 12:1)

Because God is faithful, I will trust Him to always keep His promises.

- forgives the repentant (1 John 1:9)
- God is faithful to the faithful (Dent. 7:7-11)
- God deserves thanks for His constant faithfulness (Ps. 100:5)
- God is faithful through calamity (Lam. 3:22-23)

- God faithfully matures believers (1 Thess. 5:24)
- God is faithful to fulfill His promises (Heb. 10:23)
- His faithfulness endures (Ps. 119:90)
- His faithfulness is immeasurable (Ps. 36:5)

Because God never changes, my future is secure and eternal.

- God never changes (Mal. 3:6)
- God is consistent throughout all time (Heb. 13:8)
- God is good–all the time (James 1:17)
- He doesn't lie and is true to His word (Num. 23:19)
- His love is never-ending (Lam. 3:22-23)
- though the universe will change, God never will (Ps. 102:25-27; Heb. 1:10-12)

How wonderful! It is my prayer that we'll invest time in looking up the above passages. What comfort and reassurance they bring to our hearts, minds, and lives.

The Attributes of God Associated with His Name

In the Bible when we read LORD all in uppercase, LORD is used to denote that there is a unique and distinct name of God the word LORD is being used for. Additionally, in many places in the Bible, the word 'name' is substituted for a specific given name and attribute of God.

When I read LORD in my Bible, I am alerted to the fact that some metadata exists in association with the use of the word LORD that I do not see in my reading in a given translation of the Word.

Each of the many names of God describes a different aspect of His multi-faceted character; the metadata I referred to above. There are over 200 different names used for God in the Old and New Testaments. I have not found agreement on the number in my research, but I am in awe of what I have found and read.

I like the definitions below for the word attribute. Merriam-Webster defines it as such:

1: a quality, character, or characteristic ascribed to someone or something
2: an object closely associated with or belonging to a specific person, thing, or office; a word ascribing a quality

There's a book I'd like to recommend by author Ann Spangler titled, '*The Names of God.*' I had the joy of studying her work with others in a Sunday school class a number of years ago. I owe it to myself to reread it.

God's Purpose for When He Speaks

> *"For I am jealous for you with a godly jealousy; for I betrothed you to one husband, so that to Christ I might present you as a pure virgin. But I am afraid that, as the serpent deceived Eve by his craftiness, your minds will be led astray from the simplicity and purity of devotion to Christ." (2 Corinthians 11:2-3)*

Throughout the Scriptures, we see believers pictured as a chaste Bride (the church) betrothed to the Bridegroom, Jesus Christ. God is in the process of creating a chase bride for His beloved Son. My brother, this speaks of us - of all who love the Lord.

We must allow the Spirit of God into this transformation process that we might be presented to Jesus Christ as a pure bride. This is at the heart of the battle we are in, especially as we war against the world and the flesh.

I once heard Christian comedian, Jerry Clower say, "You know, the first time I got married, I was the groom. The next time I'm gettin' married, I'm gonna be the bride!" I still smile broadly at the thought.

Satan is all about beguiling the bride of Christ today, just as the serpent beguiled Eve, the bride of Adam. Satan wants to corrupt the minds of the believers. Satan so desires to separate us away from our single-mindedness of allowing "Christ in you" to manifest Himself in us daily. He wants to shut us up.

God speaks so that we might be conformed to the image of Jesus Christ. He speaks so that we might relive the life of Jesus Christ and that we might ask others "Do you know Jesus Christ as Lord and Savior? Who do you say that He is?"

How God Speaks

God speaks to us in many ways, but primarily through His divine and precious inspired Word. The word inspired means God-breathed. But God also speaks to us through the words of others, through Godly messages we listen to on the radio, via YouTube, or elsewhere, and sometimes through thoughts that come in a moment.

God Speaks Primarily Through His Word...

> *"Your word is a lamp to my feet and a light to my path."*
> *(Psalm 119:105)*

> *"All Scripture is inspired by God* [God-breathed] *and profitable for teaching, for reproof, for correction, for training in righteousness;" (1 Timothy 3:16, insert mine)*

First and foremost, God speaks through His Word. He may do so softly, even inaudibly, and sometimes He SHOUTS so as to awaken us from our slumber.

The Word of God is always the voice of God, because all Scripture is God-breathed. He spoke and all things came into being. He moved men in ages past to put words to pen as He inspired them to do so. He used the unique qualities and character of those men to write what they did, but it was as the Spirit of God led them to do so.

God once spoke something to me through His Word by giving me a unique perspective in the passage of Scripture below (2 Corinthians 1:3-4).

*"Blessed be the God and Father of our Lord Jesus Christ, the
Father of mercies and God of all comfort, who comforts us in
all our affliction so that we will be able to comfort those who
are in any affliction with the comfort with which we ourselves
are comforted by God." (2 Corinthians 1:3-4)*

After reading and reflecting on this passage, this thought came to mind:
The truth be told, you-know-what has and will hit the fan in all of our lives.
But one of the great blessings of being in Christ is that we do not have to
smell like that which hit the fan. As a child of the King, I can smell like
Old Spice (the cologne my dad wore), and a sister in the Lord can smell like
Chanel No.5. 2 Corinthians 2:14-17 speaks wonderfully of just this truth:

*But thanks be to God, who always leads us in triumph in
Christ, and manifests through us the sweet aroma of the
knowledge of Him in every place. For we are a fragrance of
Christ to God among those who are being saved and among
those who are perishing; to the one an aroma from death to
death, to the other an aroma from life to life. And who is
adequate for these things? (2 Corinthians 2:14-16)*

My point is this: those around us that do not know Jesus Christ take note
of this aroma in us and about us. It causes them to wonder.

Now living my life in a wheelchair, I have used these passages when sharing
my gratitude to Jesus Christ for all of His goodness poured out to me
throughout my life. I have often been amazed how it has spoken to others.
Maybe I shouldn't be.

God speaks specifically to us through the Bible by drawing a particular
passage to our attention or to our recollection. This is further evidence of
the work of the indwelling Holy Spirit of God.

*"For the word of God is living and active and sharper than
any two-edged sword, and piercing as far as the division of
soul and spirit, of both joints and marrow, and able to judge
the thoughts and intentions of the heart." (Hebrews 4:12)*

God speaks to us directly and specifically through His matchless Word. We are to declare His Word to the world around us. It's not just a matter of speaking the Word of God, but the verbal declaration of the Word of God. I'm still learning to do this - to speak His Word to others and to pray it to the Lord.

God Speaks Through His Son, Jesus Christ...

> *"In the past God spoke to our forefathers through the prophets at many times and in various ways, but in these last days he has spoken to us by His Son, whom he appointed heir of all things, and through whom he made the universe"* *(Hebrews 1:1-2, NIV).*

My brother, what a powerful truth this is. Not only do we hear God speak when we read the Bible, we hear God speak when Jesus Christ speaks.

I could fill and overflow the pages of this book with Scriptures of all the things that Jesus Christ is speaking to us through the Word of Jesus. Find a red-letter Bible, referencing the spoken words of Jesus, and read it. Read the claims He has made about Himself. Read who He is! The gospel of John is loaded with the claims Jesus Christ makes about Himself.

> *"I and the Father are one." (John 10:30)*

I have always been drawn to the Book of John. There is a glorious irony in John 18:38 that I want to address about Pilate's response to Jesus, but first the passage (I've included the verse numbers for easier reference):

> *33 Therefore Pilate entered again into the Praetorium, and summoned Jesus and said to Him, "Are You the King of the Jews?" 34 Jesus answered, "Are you saying this on your own initiative, or did others tell you about Me?" 35 Pilate answered, "I am not a Jew, am I? Your own nation and the chief priests delivered You to me; what have You done?" 36 Jesus answered, "My kingdom is not of this world. If My kingdom were of this world, then My servants would be*

fighting so that I would not be handed over to the Jews; but as it is, My kingdom is not of this realm." [37] *Therefore Pilate said to Him, "So You are a king?" Jesus answered, "You say correctly that I am a king. For this I have been born, and for this I have come into the world, to testify to the truth. Everyone who is of the truth hears My voice."* [38] **Pilate *said to Him, "What is truth?"** *And when he had said this, he went out again to the Jews and said to them, "I find no guilt in Him. (John 18:33-38; emphasis mine)*

The powerful irony is this: Pilate asked, *"What is truth?"* to Truth Himself.

Again, the Book of John amplifies this in the following passage.

Jesus said to him [Thomas], *"I am the way, and the truth, and the life; no one comes to the Father but through Me. (John 14:6; insert mine)*

God Speaks Through His Creation…

For since the creation of the world His invisible attributes, His eternal power and divine nature, have been clearly seen, being understood through what has been made, so that they are without excuse. (Romans 1:20)

Even as a young child I saw the wondrous works of God all around me and even as a lost teenager I knew there had to be a God because I saw intelligent design at work. I love to recall the many physical wonders and the incredible beauty of God's creation I have seen and experienced throughout my life.

In my later teenage years I once lived with an uncle in a remote part of South Dakota - I mean dead-center in the middle of nowhere. The only other house in sight was inhabited by raccoons. When we got hungry, we hunted. When we needed money, we would capture a fox or two and sell their hides for cash.

My uncle had about a dozen Siberian Huskies that he bred, selling their strong and beautiful pups for needed cash. Often I'd hunt alone with his and my favorite dog, a half greyhound, half St. Bernard, named Butch. That animal would stand up against the front of my body and place his front paws across my shoulders and look at me eye to eye, and I'm 6'2".

However, his one animal that I was most in awe of was a full grown Timber Wolf that my uncle found when it was young. Its name was Lobo (meaning Timber Wolf). My uncle and I were the only two humans that Lobo would allow to handle him. Every morning and evening that magnificent creature would let loose with a long, loud wolf howl and the Siberian Huskies would follow suit.

I was floored the first night I heard this chorus of great animals, with a wolf in lead. It was awesome. I could not deny that something (or Someone) was at work in the world.

I've also known and loved the oceans along the east coast of Florida, southern California, Oregon, and along the Gulf Coast. I lived in Lake Tahoe – a stunningly beautiful and wondrous environment (and many people as lost and broken as I was at the time).

I recall as a child in South Florida the incredible colorations and designs I saw in the large venomous caterpillars that were in the bushes around our house, and I wondered how they got those brilliant markings. I also had instilled in me by my mom a love for rocks and minerals that I maintain to this day - all giving evidence of Intelligent Design. God is, indeed, at work revealing Himself through His creation.

While at work, I'd hand a stunning rock or a gem into the hands of any number of engineers from all across the world, and suggest to them, "My friend, intelligent design begs an Intelligent Designer."

I've had some interesting responses to that statement. Most of them carefully returned the rock to my hand saying, "Thank you very much, Mr. Steve," before quickly darting out of my office. They knew what I was suggesting. I believe they, too, saw His hand at work in what they held in their hand.

God Speaks Through Other believers...

> *Therefore encourage one another and build up one another, just as you also are doing. (1 Thessalonians 5:11)*

I am grateful to the Lord to have known a great number of dear saints, friends who met the above description. They were encouragers. I have also been blessed through the years to have been a member of churches with pastors that loved our Lord and risen Savior, Jesus Christ, and knew the Word of God. I was well-fed early on in my walk. I learned from them, and by the power of the indwelling Holy Spirit, to feed myself.

God Speaks Through His Holy Spirit...

> *"In the same way the Spirit also helps our weakness; for we do not know how to pray as we should, but the Spirit Himself intercedes for us with groanings too deep for words; and He who searches the hearts knows what the mind of the Spirit is, because He intercedes for the saints according to the will of God." (Romans 8:26-27)*

Not only does the Holy Spirit speak to us, He prays for us on our behalf.

> *"Do you not know that you are a temple of God and that the Spirit of God dwells in you?" (1 Corinthians 3:16)*

The Holy Spirit speaks to us with that still small voice. Sometimes He speaks to us through a thought that comes in a moment, or He brings to mind a biblical passage, so as to redirect our feelings, our thinking, or our actions - or all three.

God Speaks Through Prayer...

> *"Be anxious for nothing, but in everything by prayer and supplication with thanksgiving let your requests be made known to God. And the peace of God, which surpasses all comprehension, will guard your hearts and your minds in Christ Jesus." (Philippians 4:6-7)*

Prayer is direct address to God. Prayer is communication between the human soul and the God who created it. It is not formulaic - it isn't to be engaged in by the mouthing of words we've learned or heard from others. It is one-to-One communication with Almighty God.

Prayer is the way we share our desires, our struggles, our emotions, our fears, our failures, and our requests with God. Through prayer and praise is how we best express our thanksgiving to God; our gratitude for His unfailing love and His divine provision in our lives. We can praise Him and tell Him how much we love Him in prayer. I have found that true communication with God in prayer requires periods of silence while I pray.

True communication is two-sided. We both speak to God and we listen. There should be a selah element in our praying - that moment when we are silent before Him and we allow Him to speak to us by way of His Holy Spirit.

Jesus Christ is our greatest example of one who was in constant prayer with His Father. Allow the Scriptures below to speak to your heart.

> *"After He had sent the crowds away, He went up on the mountain by Himself to pray; and when it was evening, He was there alone." (Matthew 14:23)*

> *"It was at this time that He went off to the mountain to pray, and He spent the whole night in prayer to God." (Luke 6:12)*

"In the early morning, while it was still dark, Jesus got up, left the house, and went away to a secluded place, and was praying there." (Mark 1:35)

"But Jesus Himself would often slip away to the wilderness and pray." (Luke 5:16)

And He went a little beyond them, and fell on His face and prayed, saying, "My Father, if it is possible, let this cup pass from Me; yet not as I will, but as You will." (Matthew 26:39)

If our Lord and Savior was daily in prayer before His Father, how much more so should we be.

When I read the Matthew 26:39 passage above, *"And He went a little beyond them…",* it speaks to me that He, Jesus, went beyond human companionship. He went directly to His Father. I believe this is the heart of prayer for us - a direct one to One communication with Almighty God.

Prayer is about the heart of a man and the will of God for him.

What Does it Mean to Hear God Speak?

Hearing God speak may mean different things to different people. As a parent, I saw that my two daughters were unique, distinct, and precious individuals. I would address each differently, even when it pertained to a similar issue. God sees each of us, His children, in the same way; that each of us is unique and distinct creations. There is no doubt that God speaks to each of us in unique ways, in ways that speak directly, distinctly, and clearly to us.

When you sense that God has been, or is silent in your life, ask yourself this: were you obedient last time He spoke? If not, why would He choose to speak again? Not obeying and delayed obedience are both disobedience. Additionally, I believe there are times in our lives when God trusts us with His silence. We are to come to Him by faith, not based on what we feel or think in the moment.

When God Speaks Through Others

God spoke to David through the court prophet, Nathan.

> *Nathan then said to David, "You are the man! Thus says the Lord God of Israel, 'It is I who anointed you king over Israel and it is I who delivered you from the hand of Saul. I also gave you your master's house and your master's wives into your care, and I gave you the house of Israel and Judah; and if that had been too little, I would have added to you many more things like these! Why have you despised the word of the Lord by doing evil in His sight? You have struck down Uriah the Hittite with the sword, have taken his wife to be your wife, and have killed him with the sword of the sons of Ammon. (II Samuel 12:7–9)*

God spoke to the Ethiopian eunuch through Phillip.

> *"But an angel of the Lord spoke to Philip saying, "Get up and go south to the road that descends from Jerusalem to Gaza." So he got up and went; and there was an Ethiopian eunuch, a court official of Candace, queen of the Ethiopians, who was in charge of all her treasure; and he had come to Jerusalem to worship, and he was returning and sitting in his chariot, and was reading the prophet Isaiah. Then the Spirit said to Philip, "Go up and join this chariot." Philip ran up and heard him reading Isaiah the prophet, and said, "Do you understand what you are reading?" And he said, "Well, how could I, unless someone guides me?" And he invited Philip to come up and sit with him. (Acts 8:26-31)*

Throughout the Word of God, God speaks through others. In the Old Testament He spoke through angels, through prophets, and even through a donkey (full account in Numbers 22:21-38). That's encouragement to me.

> *When the donkey saw the angel of the Lord, she lay down under Balaam; so Balaam was angry and struck the donkey*

with his stick. And the Lord opened the mouth of the donkey, and she said to Balaam, "What have I done to you, that you have struck me these three times?" (Numbers 22:27-28)

When God personally spoke to me through another...

God does indeed speak to us through others in our lives. I want to offer a testimony about a couple of times when God spoke personally, specifically, and uniquely to me.

There was a night during a dark and very challenging period in my life and walk with Jesus Christ when I both heard the Spirit of God speak and knew it was Him speaking. It was during a time of employment heartbreak and financial challenges that seemed overwhelming at the time. I saw no end to either.

On that particular night I found myself wrestling with God, asking "Why?" and demanding an answer. God was silent.

As I struggled to make sense of my emotions and what I was feeling, it was as if I found myself beginning to despair. It was a tornado-like spiritual spiral downward, even to the point of questioning my belief in God.

I had begun to wonder if God really cared about me or my family or if He had a plan for my life. I even began to doubt if He was real. I felt as if I was dying spiritually. There was little if any sense of hope in me.

At that moment I was suddenly aware that my young daughter, Sarah (about age 4 at the time), was standing at the foot of our bed. My wife was sound asleep. This was highly unusual. Sarah never got out of bed at night. She would usually call out to either her mother or me to come to her if she had want or need of something.

"Sarah," I asked, "What are you doing out of bed?"

She said, verbatim, this: "Daddy, Jesus is happy in my heart because I don't doubt."

That was all she spoke.

I gasped. I got up, reached out to her and gathered her into my arms. She was sound asleep before I entered her bedroom. I wept grateful tears as I walked back to my bedroom. I remember thinking that I did not ever recall using the word doubt in context with her.

My doubt had been settled. In my journal account of that night I titled it 'No Doubt.' I remember this like it happened yesterday. Yes, that night, God spoke to me through my four-year old daughter. I heard Him speak to me through her.

God Speaks through thoughts and words that come to us in a moment

It was Christmas Day, 2000 and the divorce I went through was over. It was a heartbreaking divorce that I neither wanted, nor asked for. I was finally in an apartment and my beloved younger daughter, Micah, was living with me. On that Christmas day, both daughters were at their mother's condo to celebrate with her, and I was alone in my apartment. And I do not believe I have ever felt as alone as I did then.

While in the kitchen, I lowered myself to the ground and curled tightly into a near fetal position. For a period of time, I just laid there and wept. At some point, I verbally cried out to God, "I'm so lonely!" It was an incredibly bitter and hurtful cry. Almost immediately, I heard or sensed this audibly: "I want you to want Me."

Initially I was stunned - afraid. I opened my eyes, quickly got off the floor, and listened, wondering if the maintenance man had maybe let himself in to repair my wall heater. I walked around the corner to look. No one was there but me, but I was not alone.

As I repeated aloud what I had heard, I smiled. It was as if a song had come to mind, as if a song named "I Want You to Want Me" had just played, but in a distinctly unique and personal way. There was no music, just the words.

A peace enveloped me. That peace carried me wonderfully through that Christmas day - what a peace - His Peace.

> *You shall not bow down before them or serve them. For I, the LORD, your God, am a jealous God, inflicting punishment for their ancestors' wickedness on the children of those who hate me, down to the third and fourth generation; (Exodus 20:5)*

He wants us to want Him. He is a jealous God. He is jealous for us and for me, and He speaks this to me to this day. "I want you to want Me."

God Speaks Through Dreams and Visions

God may choose to speak to us through dreams and visions. Worldly news tells us nothing of the countless many people of other cultures and faiths that testify that they have seen Jesus in a vision or a dream.

> *"It will come about after this that I will pour out My Spirit on all mankind; and your sons and daughters will prophesy, your old men will dream dreams, your young men will see visions." (Joel 2:28)*

I must state this regarding dreams and visions - a great deal of discernment must be exercised in the church regarding the issue of one hearing God speak through either of these two manners.

I've heard and read of people sharing such, only to make what they either heard or experienced (or think they heard or experienced) something that trumps what the Word of God proclaims. It is as if they begin to preach what they heard or saw – preaching 'something new.' It can so easily become out of bounds. Yet, I must share of another time I heard the Spirit of God speak to me.

When the Spirit of God spoke distinctly to me...

> *And he said to all, "If anyone would come after me, let him deny himself and take up his cross daily and follow me."* *(Luke 9:23)*

In spring of 1988, while attending an Easter special from the balcony of the wonderful church I attended then, I had an experience. My then wife, daughter, and I were seated in the balcony. That evening as I watched the passion story being dramatically played out before me, I suddenly lost sight of the stage. All I knew initially was that my body felt as if it was being pushed down to my left. It felt as if someone strong, or something heavy, was pushing down on my left shoulder.

Then I felt something rough and scratchy to the left side of my face. I began to feel pain from the weight of it. It was a cross! It was rougher and heavier then I had imagined. I found myself bent down towards the direction of my left knee at its weight, and for a moment I was aware only of it - the cross and me.

The next thing I realized was that it was as if I was on my knees before the throne of God, with a cross on my shoulder. I was petrified. "This doesn't happen in church, does it?" Faint words and tears came from within me as I asked silently, "What do I do now, Lord? What do I do with this rough and heavy cross?"

Then I heard in my spirit, "Carry it unto death."

About then, my wife pushed on me and gave me an irritated and quizzical look. She never asked about it, nor about the tears in my eyes, and I did not share that moment later with her. Maybe I should have…

In reference to the nature of the cross, A.W. Tozer, in his book, '*The Pursuit of God*,' states the following: "The cross is rough and it is deadly, but it is effective." The Lord commands us to take up our cross and follow Him (Matthew 16:24 & Luke 9:23). We are to deny ourselves, take up our cross and follow Him - what a call!

Tozer nails it when he says, "The cross is rough and deadly, but it does not keep its victim hanging there forever. There comes an hour when its work is finished and the suffering victim dies. After death comes resurrection glory and power." This section reads to me like poetry.

The author is right when he says we stop fooling ourselves when we accept God's estimate of us and of our lives. What supernatural power there is when we realize that the world will never see us as God sees us, and that we can rest in that.

Carry it unto death.

Dr. Harold J. Sala, through Guidelines International Ministries, in a five-minute devotional titled "How Do I Hear the Voice of God?" speaks the following:

"God's voice is too often drowned out by a thousand other voices that clamor for our time and recognition. Want to hear His voice more clearly? Take time to read His letters to you in the Bible. Take time to meditate on what you have learned, and listen to His voice in prayer. The voice of God is saying, "Here's the path to real heaven. Here's the way to life." Only a fool would deafen his ears to that kind of a voice."

Regarding Discernment

My, brothers, I have shared a number of personal experiences with you. The experiences I have shared are a part of my personal testimony as a Christian, as a child of the King. But I must exercise Godly caution with you about what I have shared. My hope and faith is found in my relationship with Jesus Christ - in Him only.

I do not know why I have experienced, or seen, or heard the sights and the words I've written of. I have kept many of these experiences close to myself in the past, but I believe I have been led to share what I have experienced in this writing.

I know of a number of times when others have spoken publicly about visions and words spoken to them from God. There have been times I was grieved in the Spirit when I heard such words spoken. Discernment is highly subjective in nature. Again, Godly discernment is a must.

Yet, again, how can I not but share these things?

God speaks most clearly and most directly to us through His inspired Word - through His God-breathed Word. All things - thoughts, words, and deeds - are to be exposed to and examined by the Word of God. God is not the author of confusion - our enemy is.

The Word of God is our marching orders. May we each be in it daily, so we will know and carry out the great tasks He has for us. Amen.

Study Guide - Chapter 5

Day 1

a) What personal encouragement do you find in the phrase, *"This is what the LORD of Heaven's Armies says"*?

b) When God speaks, do you listen? Have you "heard" Him speak? Capture a memory or two.

Responses:

c) In the section **Qualities of God - the Attributes Associated with His Name**, what three attributes of God bring you the most comfort and peace? State why.

d) One of the given definitions of attribute is this: a word ascribing a quality. Take a moment and pen a few of the qualities of God as you see Him?

Responses:

Day 2

a) What does it mean to you that the Word of God is inspired - 'God-breathed?' State what that means to you in your own words.

b) How should the Bible being "God-breathed' affect our embrace of the Bible?

Responses:

c) Read the passage below from Hebrews and reflect upon it for a moment. Capture a few thoughts about what this passage means to you.

d) What does it personally say to you?

"For the word of God is living and active and sharper than any two-edged sword, and piercing as far as the division of soul and spirit, of both joints and marrow, and able to judge the thoughts and intentions of the heart." (Hebrews 4:12)

Responses:

Day 3

Passage: *For since the creation of the world His invisible attributes, His eternal power and divine nature, have been clearly seen, being understood through what has been made, so that they are without excuse. (Romans 1:20)*

a) Romans 1:20 speaks of how God is seen in and through His creation. When and where were you when you have seen God revealed through His creation? Speak of the wonders you have seen.

b) Which of these revelations meant the most to you at the time - and why?

Response:

Day 4

    a)   The passages below were included in this chapter without any commentary associated with them. Read each and provide some of your thoughts about them.

    b)   How do they speak personally to you.

    c)   What encouragement do you find in each?

Passage: *"I have told you these things, so that in me you may have peace. In this world you will have trouble. But take heart! I have overcome the world." (John 16:33)*

Response:

Day 5

    a)   The passages below were included in this chapter without any commentary associated with them. Read each and provide some of your thoughts about them.

    b)   How do they speak personally to you.

    c)   What encouragement do you find in each?

Passage: *Now it came about when Joshua was by Jericho, that he lifted up his eyes and looked, and behold, a man was standing opposite him with his sword drawn in his hand, and Joshua went to him and said to him, "Are you for us or for our adversaries?" 14 He said, "No; rather I indeed come now as captain of the host of the Lord." And Joshua fell on his face to the earth, and bowed down, and said to him, "What has my lord to say to his servant?" (Joshua 5:13-14)*

What is the Lord saying to you through this passage from Joshua?

Response:

Passage: *For His lovingkindness is great toward us, and the truth of the Lord is everlasting. Praise the Lord! (Psalm 117:2)*

<u>Response:</u>

Passage: *"He said, "No; rather I indeed come now as captain of the host of the LORD." And Joshua fell on his face to the earth, and bowed down, and said to him, "What has my lord to say to his servant?" (Joshua 5:14)*

<u>Response:</u>

Chapter 6

ARISE!

"He who has the seven Spirits of God and the seven stars, says this: 'I know your deeds, that you have a name that you are alive, but you are dead. Wake up, and strengthen the things that remain, which were about to die; for I have not found your deeds completed in the sight of My God. So remember what you have received and heard; and keep it, and repent. Therefore if you do not wake up, I will come like a thief, and you will not know at what hour I will come to you." (Revelation 3:1-3)

Wake up

> *"Wake up and strengthen the things that remain, which were about to die." (Revelation 3:2)*

I've heard it said that the tough thing about being a living sacrifice is that we tend to crawl off the altar. I have experienced this repeatedly in my walk with Jesus Christ. I recognize that the point here is that our old nature is tough to put to death. It's a daily battle.

No doubt we Christian men, at one period of time or another, have dropped the ball on our walk with Jesus Christ. We've gone AWOL (absent without leave). This doesn't necessarily imply desertion, but rather that we are not where we're supposed to be and not doing what we're supposed to be doing.

We can so easily retreat to our former ways - even to the very caves we once lived in, so as to isolate ourselves from the world around us - to once again become self-absorbed.

Remember, Satan desires to isolate us. We are easier to pick off when we are alone. When we're not in fellowship with God and other believers, we open ourselves to his attacks.

I read the Revelation 3:1-3 passage as a call to re-enlist; to reawaken.

Falling Away - Leaving our First Love

> *"The One who holds the seven stars in His right hand, the One who walks among the seven golden lampstands, says this: 'I know your deeds and your toil and perseverance, and that you cannot tolerate evil men, and you put to the test those who call themselves apostles, and they are not, and you found them to be false; and you have perseverance and have endured for My name's sake, and have not grown weary. **But I have this against you, that you have left your first love. Therefore remember from where you have fallen, and repent and do the deeds you did at first; or else I am coming to you and will remove your lampstand out of its place—unless you repent.** (Revelation 2:1-5, emphasis mine)*

In the early years in my faith walk with Jesus Christ, I was in college full time, and I worked nights at two different restaurants as a waiter. I also mowed yards on the weekends for diaper and milk money. My wife was a fulltime mom, and I had my two precious daughters that I dearly loved, played with, and prayed for daily. Needless to say, I was busy.

Yet, after family related activities, dinner, cleaning up, tucking my daughters in, and studying the material I was learning in college - every night I would spend lengthy times in the Word and in prayer - flat on my face on the floor. In the morning as I left for school, I could see an outline of the carpet angel I made the night before while lying flat on the thick shag carpeting as I praised God and prayed.

Yes, times were tough, but there was a daily drive in my spirit to know more about the Word, to know the Bible better, and to pray as if my entire life depended upon it. And it did.

Others saw the challenges and hardships both myself and my family experienced. A well-meaning Christian friend back then even asked me, "Are you guys cursed?" Of course we weren't, but it was obvious to me that my life differed greatly from many of my Christian friend's lives at the time.

Looking back at those days, I recognize that it was open season on me. The enemy was working overtime to derail me from my pursuit of God. The truth be told, I have had to take captive the memory of the words of my Christian friend. Believe me; Satan has had some fun with me with the words, "are you guys cursed?"

But when and where did I leave that first love? How did it become lost to me? When was the last time I left a visual reminder of an extended time in prayer and praise? I ask myself, "Where has it gone from my life?" No doubt, over time, there are dozens of things and circumstances that I've allowed to rob me of it. I have found that when you forget how good that first love is, you, in time, forget to nurture it.

> *"So because you are lukewarm, and neither hot nor cold, I will spit you out of My mouth." (Revelation 3:16)*

In this passage God is saying, "I will reject you from my innermost being!" We do this very thing when we vomit, because something we have eaten is foul. Our stomach rejects it forcibly. The Word of God says the same about those of us who are, or have grown lukewarm, in our love for Christ. The state of being lukewarm points to a loss of one's first love.

Where are you - right now - with the Lord? Surely you know. If you have not yet come to saving faith in Jesus Christ, my friend, there is no better time than now.

If you have accepted Jesus Christ as Lord and Savior, but over time you have fallen away from Him, is it time for you to re-enlist? Truth be told, re-enlistment into God's army needs to happen from time to time throughout the different seasons of our lives.

My brother, have you left or lost your first love? Has the presence and power of the gospel of Jesus Christ grown cold in your life? That distancing ourselves from our Savior can happen as we begin to place our focus on our circumstances, rather than on our victory stance in Jesus Christ. This has happened numerous times in my life.

The message of the book of James is addressed specifically to believers who are inclined to talk their way to heaven rather than to walk their way there, and a world of difference exists between the two. Re-enlistment for a Christian who has lost his first love is much like repentance. It is a change of heart and mind, AND a change of direction.

Eight Steps of Repentance for the Worldly Believer

We all have times in our Christian walk with the Lord when we need to repent from the things that have crowded out our first love for God.

There are four excellent verses in the book of James (4:7-10) that flesh out what re-enlistment entails. When I first taught this passage, I titled it 'The Eight Steps of Repentance for the Worldly Believer.' It clearly speaks to re-enlistment. Here's the passage.

> *"Submit therefore to God. Resist the devil and he will flee from you. Draw near to God and He will draw near to you. Cleanse your hands, you sinners; and purify your hearts, you double-minded. Be miserable and mourn and weep; let your laughter be turned into mourning and your joy to gloom.*

Humble yourselves in the presence of the Lord, and He will exalt you." (James 4:7-10)

The body of Christ needs to be made up of and strengthened by men and women who remain faithful in the face of difficult trials, temptations, and circumstances. These three challenges, and many others, want to rob us of the power of God in our lives.

The enemy of our souls wants to thwart us. He wants to wreck us and to derail us so as to halt our forward movement in Christ. We must recognize that we are weak and prone to leave the one we love.

Chapter 4 of James talks of wars and fights amongst us. Verse 6 closes with, "God resists the proud, but gives grace to the humble." That's where He extends His loving hand in the verses to follow to help draw us back to Himself.

Vs. 7a "Therefore, submit to God…"

Submission: the true starting point for any/all repentant believers - the umbrella under which the following seven steps reside.

- Submitting in this instance is essentially renouncing rebellion
- Surrender: Open hands raised into the air, dropping *(letting go of)* all we had held in them prior. It is in essence saying, *"Lord, I surrender."*

Vs. 7b "resist the devil and he will flee from you."

Resist: There are supernatural forces that tempt man and that draw us out from under the cover of God. As God opposes the proud, we are to oppose Satan.

Point: "Resist the devil and he will flee;" what a beautiful biblical promise.

Vs. 8a "Draw near to God and He will draw near to you."

Draw near to God: Psalm 145:18, *"God is near to all who call upon Him."* This verse speaks to me of how a frightened child cries out for his daddy or mommy for protection, comfort and security.

Vs. 8b "Cleanse your hands, you sinners"

Cleanse: Hands represents our outward life - the spiritual cleansing of the instruments of sin. God, through James, is saying, *"wash your hands of the act."* Whatever the act is that takes our focus off of Jesus Christ.

Vs. 8c "and purify your hearts, you double-minded."

Purify: Outward cleansing alone never suffices. Inward purity alone pleases God. Double-minded, in the Greek, means to be two-souled – one foot in the world and the other in spiritual matters.

Verse 8c, in the New Living Translation, reads - *purify your hearts, **for your loyalty is divided between God and the world.** (James 4: 8 – NLT; emphasis mine)*

The point here is that clean hands receive their life's blood from a pure heart. It's always about the heart.

Vs. 9a "Lament and mourn and weep"

We are to feel and express sorrow or regret over our sins. This phrase states that we are to feel our sorrow deeply when we realize our spiritual condition. "Look what I've come to, Lord!" as we cry out to Him. James calls us to feel grief (in Greek, to grieve means to carve deeply) when the worldly Christian realizes how far he or she has strayed.

Wretchedness is not a room to live in, but a door to pass through on the way to renewed fellowship. Perpetual wretchedness would be like trying to run a marathon with a ball and chain around your ankle. Good luck with that.

We are to ask God to forgive us. We then ask the offended one to forgive us and additionally, I have found that I need to forgive myself. I heard Pastor Tony Evans say this on the radio, "You can't drive forward while looking in the rearview mirror." It is so easy to allow the stain of shame to hinder our forward movement in Christ. Satan is the great accuser of the faithful. He lies because he is the Liar.

For too many years in my life, I often carried around a big stick that I would spiritually hit myself with. One evening in prayer, I was lamenting past sins before the Lord, ones I had already confessed and repented of. Then, in the still of the moment, the words, "Put down the big stick you hit yourself with" came to me. There was a wonderful release in that moment.

We are to feel miserable guilt for only as long as it takes to repent. That inner sense of wretchedness usually has an outward display in the way of an emotional response. To feel deeply about something, we are to respond deeply to it. Don't let the past direct your thinking. Embrace God's forgiveness and move on.

Adrian Rogers offers an excellent word through his Love Worth Finding Ministries online devotional that speaks directly about living in the present. It's titled "Two days that will Steal Your Joy."

"Brethren, I count not myself to have apprehended: but this one thing I do, forgetting those things which are behind, and reaching forth unto those things which are before, I press toward the mark for the prize of the high calling of God in Christ Jesus." (Philippians. 3:13-14)

There are two days that can steal your joy and the fulfillment of today. One is tomorrow and the other is yesterday. Both are days in which we as Christians should refuse to live.

So many of us have never learned how to separate ourselves from yesterday. We are still dragging it around with us and it is stealing our joy. Paul could have lived there in the realm of guilt, but he refused.

Maybe you, like Paul and countless others, have committed some horrible sins. But friend, what God has called cleaned, let no man call unclean. If you have confessed that sin and given it to God, it is buried in the depths. Don't let it contaminate your day. Learn to live in the present.

Let's continue our look at James 4:7-10.

Vs. 9b "Let your laughter be turned to mourning and your joy into gloom."

Radical Reversal: Laughter, in the Greek, references a feast of fools who have declared independence from God. Laughter, as if at a bar or nightclub - our loud, raucous, pleasure-loving laughter turns into quiet introspection when we finally come to our spiritual senses. James is saying that there should be a marked contrast to previous behavior by the repentant believer.

Vs. 10 "Humble yourself in the sight of the Lord, and He will lift you up."

Humble yourself: These eight steps to repentance conclude as they began - the matter of one submitting himself/herself to God. Humble yourself before God and He will exalt you. Lower yourself before God, and He will lift you up.

The Apostle Peter's Re-enlistment

All four gospel accounts address Peter's denial of Jesus Christ on the night before His execution on Calvary, but only the gospel of John speaks on Jesus' re-enlistment of Peter. (For reference, the four accounts of Peter's denial can be found in Matthew 26:69-75, Mark 14:66-72, Luke 22:54-62, and John 18:15-27.)

We find the re-enlistment account in John 21:15-17. But before we look at it, I want to offer some thoughts I have entertained about this passage, beginning with verses 1-3 of John 21.

> *After these things Jesus manifested Himself again to the disciples at the Sea of Tiberias, and He manifested Himself in this way. Simon Peter, and Thomas called Didymus, and Nathanael of Cana in Galilee, and the sons of Zebedee, and two others of His disciples were together. Simon Peter said to them,* **"I am going fishing."** *They said to him, "We will also come with you." They went out and got into the boat;* **and that night they caught nothing.** *(John 21:1-3; emphasis mine)*

"And that night they caught nothing;" I've known such nights (and days) while fishing, have you?

At this moment, these men return to what they knew naturally. They were fisherman, had some down time, and needed both food and maybe a source of revenue. It is very likely that Peter needed some form of escape from the great disappointment and shame he felt within himself after His denials of knowing Jesus.

Peter's Nature...

Peter was an impulsive man who was inclined to open his mouth without re-engaging his brain. Truly, he had done just that the night he denied Jesus three times, just as Jesus told Peter he would - read Luke 22:31-34. Peter had problems in the following areas:

- He was over confident and boastful: he wanted to prove his ability to follow Jesus anywhere, regardless.
- He talked a lot (open mouth and insert foot, or open mouth and swap feet).
- He often failed to pray - in Gethsemane and elsewhere.
- He was impulsive and tended to react in the moment.

My question to each of us is this: Who amongst us hasn't struggled in the same or similar ways? But Peter loved Jesus, and at every opportunity he wanted to be close to Him.

Peter's Profession...

Peter was a fisherman before Jesus called him. John 4:18-19 says:

> *Now as Jesus was walking by the Sea of Galilee, He saw two brothers, Simon who was called Peter, and Andrew his brother, casting a net into the sea; for they were fishermen. And He said to them, "Follow Me, and I will make you fishers of men." (John 4:18-19)*

Jesus' Question - "Simon, do you love me?"

Three times in the following John 21:15-17 passages, Jesus asks, *"Simon, do you love Me?"* See Peter seated there with Jesus, while around a fire of coals, and after a miraculous catch of fish. Peter knew who he was. He knew deeply of his failure.

What kind of love is it that Jesus asks Simon Peter about?

Although there is a similarity in the three times Jesus asks this question. I consider these exchanges as interrogations. The three questions asked by Jesus could be considered parts of an interview for the role Jesus desired for Peter to fulfill.

There's an insightful exchange in the John 21:15-17 passages below that we can so easily miss because the word love in the passages are actually two completely different types of love being spoken of. These two words for love are phileo and agape.

Phileo: meaning friendship. This type of love has to do with the emotions and affections in human relationship, and is used in scripture as noted in the John 21:15-17 passage to follow.

Agape: This is the highest and noblest word for love. It is a divine word used to speak of the love of God. It is a great word of dignity - that our Holy God so loves, agapes, us. This type of love should astound us.

I've inserted the appropriate Greek word describing the specific type of love being spoken of in the Scriptures below.

> *¹⁵ So when they had finished breakfast, Jesus said to Simon Peter, "Simon, son of John, do you love [**agape**] Me more than these?" He said to Him, "Yes, Lord; You know that I love [**phileo**] You." He said to him, "Tend My lambs." ¹⁶ He said to him again a second time, "Simon, son of John, do you love [**agape**] Me?" He said to Him, "Yes, Lord; You know that I love [**phileo**] You." He said to him, "Shepherd My sheep." ¹⁷ He said to him the third time, "Simon, son of John, do you love [**phileo**] Me?" Peter was grieved because He said to him the third time, "Do you love [**phileo**] Me?" And he said to Him, "Lord, You know all things; You know that I love [**phileo**] You." Jesus said to him, "Tend My sheep. (John 21:15-17, inserts mine)*

You know what, the Lord Jesus Christ accepted Peter just as he was. As we read ahead into the Book of Acts and 1ˢᵗ and 2ⁿᵈ Peter, we see Peter's love deepened, and he wrote of agape in these later biblical letters - from his pen and his heart.

I also find it interesting that Jesus calls him Simon, not Peter (see John 1:42). Peter means a stone - a rock. Cephas is the Aramaic word for "rock man," and in Greek it is "Petros." But at this moment, there is still a question about Peter, so Jesus reminds him of his old name and his old nature.

In Peter's second response (which was the same as his first response), Simon replied "Yes, Lord, You know that I phileo You." It is as if he is afraid to make a declaration of agape love. He remembers his past all too well. I think we should admire him for this.

I believe at the heart of these three questions is that love for the Savior is the prerequisite for service.

From the shore, Jesus asks them *"Children, you do not have any fish, do you?"* Someday, Jesus Christ is bound to ask each of us this very question; "Did you catch anything while you were down there on earth?"

Peter, a fisherman, became the fisher of men that Jesus called him to be. He calls us to the same. Jesus re-enlisted Peter.

My brother, is it time for you to re-enlist into service to and for the Glory of God? I will never forget the day I did. I consider the following to be my first re-enlistment. There have been others.

My Re-enlistment

The Sunday morning (sometime in February 1982) that I walked the aisle and went forward at my church, I did so only because my wife, much to my surprise, stepped out first. I thought, "Man, if she goes, I go." Certainly I had come to the understanding that I was a sinner and that I needed a Savior, but there was ZERO victory in my life for the following 13 months after that day. I was in church on Sunday and right back in Adam on Monday. My old nature continued its rule and reign over my life.

Was I saved at that moment? I believe I was, because God knows my heart then and now, but there was no victory over my old nature - none. Both my old nature, and Satan, clung tightly to the territory each had forged within me.

I felt broken and confused from that day forward. Months later, late one night at home, I was in deep broken prayer to God. I felt like whatever was supposed to have happened to me that past February didn't work for me. I felt as if I were the exception. I even told God that I didn't even feel like I needed Him. I couldn't believe that I said that to Him in prayer, and I sat on the barstool in my kitchen and wept at those words. The lights I noticed on our Christmas tree brought no color to my life at that moment.

After I calmed a bit, it was as if these words were spoken to my spirit: "You've never needed anyone." That thought shocked me, but in retrospect

I knew it was true. I'd lived a very independent life up to that point, but that was about to change.

For the few months that followed, it seemed every Sunday at church I was under incredible conviction. I wondered, "Why do I feel this? What is this about?

One Sunday morning in early March 1983, I purposely stood on the front row of the church such that all I had to do was fall forward and my chin would have landed on the carpeted podium before me. I wasn't sure why I was so drawn for the need to do so, to go forward again. But, then again, why such strong conviction to do so?

To one side of me was my dear buddy, Vince. To the other side of me was a young man that the church had directed to me. He was in a 12-step program, and for some reason the church thought I could serve as a mentor or an encourager to him. Man, I had them fooled.

Then came the invitation, and I stood fixed in place. To this day, I have never heard so many stanzas of Just as I Am sung. Then, as I began to step forward, it was as if a pair of hands came up from the floor and grabbed tightly onto both of my ankles. I stood frozen in place.

I began to perspire and felt a sense of near panic. It was as if I could not willfully move.

Once the service concluded, I made a quick exit and hurriedly walked my way out to the large school bus I drove in the bus ministry. As I reached for the clipboard from the bus ministry leader's hand - the one with the names of the children on my bus - the leader of the bus ministry looked at me and asked, "Steve, are you alright?"

I didn't know anything was obvious, and in spite of my repeated attempts to assure him I was fine, he refused to allow me to drive the bus. That morning, he drove my route for me. I then quickly caught up with my wife and daughter, and drove home together.

That afternoon, I drove the three of us to my dad's home to celebrate his birthday. I was antsy the whole time there - extremely restless. All I could think about was the coming 6:00 p.m. service that evening.

Almost in mid-conversation with my dad, I stopped speaking and quickly whisked my wife and daughter into my truck, and we flew back to our home. My dad later told me that he wondered, "Where is that boy in such a hurry to get to?" I made it to the 6:00 p.m. service alone.

That evening I sat on a pew between two precious elderly women with whom I served in a second grade class they taught. As I sat there, I wrote up a list of the things I was going to give to God at the altar. Nothing and no one was going to stop me.

When the invitation was given, I immediately sprang up and began to weep as I walked across the pew aisle and hurried to the front of the sanctuary. I couldn't help the tears. My heart was wonderfully broken.

To this day I do not know how long I was up there, but I do remember the last thing I read from the list I took with me. They were these words: "Lord, I don't even know how to match my socks, let alone make important decisions in my life. I give You all of me!" And I remained on my knees and in tears at the altar for an unknown length of time.

Finally, I stood up. It was as if I needed a beach towel to blow my nose with, but I felt light as a feather. As I walked back to the row I had been seated on, my gaze was drawn back towards the altar. Huh?!

What greeted my eyes was the sight of an old, dried-up, human-sized corn husk that had been left in the sun for weeks, but there was no cob in it. I saw it as being my old self that died while on my knees and on my face before the Lord. The vision rocked me. I could draw a picture of it even now.

Still somewhat overwhelmed at the vision, I quickly looked away as I began to make my way back down the pew to my seat.

Half wondering about what I'd just seen, I cautiously returned my glance to my right towards the altar where I had bowed. When I did, I saw something completely different. The entire sanctuary platform was a strikingly beautiful, calm, reflective pool of water. I even saw the reflection of the baptistry that was above the altar platform.

Again, I was struck at what I saw, but also fully aware of the people hugging me and touching my shoulders as I returned to my seat. Their eyes and faces were aglow, and each embraced me when the service ended.

I cannot, in human terms, understand or explain the two visions. I can only express them in words. **But I was changed that evening!**

The moment I stepped into my home that night, my wife looked at me and said, "What happened?" The next day at work, the guys I worked with asked, "Newby, what's up with you?" I could not help but speak the name of Jesus Christ to them, even if I had to yell it while on the back of a friend's motorcycle as we headed to lunch.

So what happened? Bottom line: I had known for some time that I was a sinner and that I needed a Savior, but I had not, until that night, made Jesus Christ, Lord. The word lord means the right to rule. Sovereignty is never in question. Jesus is both Savior and Lord, and He must be both in our lives.

As an aside, I wept so bitterly at the altar that night that I developed a severe sinus infection. Upon seeing my doctor, he stated that because I had had a number of back to back sinus infections in the past, he feared I might become immune to antibiotics, so he prescribed a different treatment which, over a length of many months, caused my white cell count to climb so high that it took out my pancreas. I had become a type 1 diabetic.

There is much I could share about this time, but one of the most important pieces is the following. Up until then, the only thing I ever really feared was needles. I thought about just that the first day I walked into the local pharmacy to pick up my prescription of insulin and… needles. I smiled within as I walked towards the counter and silently asked, "God, why have you given me diabetes?" Expecting nothing, these words came to my mind. "I didn't give you diabetes. I've allowed it in your life to teach you discipline." I stopped and thought on those words. To this day, God is still about just that in my life – disciplining me, pruning me.

The Pivotal Question in the Word of God

> *Now when Jesus came into the district of Caesarea Philippi, He was asking His disciples, "Who do people say that the Son of Man is?" And they said, "Some say John the Baptist; and others, Elijah but still others, Jeremiah, or one of the prophets." He said to them, **"But who do you say that I am?"** Simon Peter answered, "You are the Christ, the Son of the living God." (Matthew 16:13-16; emphasis mine)*

There is no more powerful a question posed in the Word of God than this: "Who do you say that I am?" I had answered that question on my knees at the altar.

I've heard it said that Jesus can only be one of the following four: He is either legend, lunatic, liar, or He is Lord. I cannot think of a fifth option, and I am not just speaking in an alliterative sense.

Jesus asked His disciples this question, "But who do you say that I am?" just after having just fed the 4,000. As the disciples had gathered the leftovers from among the crowd, they no doubt, heard what the people were saying about Him. Now that Jesus and His disciples had withdrawn from the masses, He had the opportunity to pose this question to them. He asks that of us to this day. All of eternity rests on our response to it.

"But who do you say that I am?"

Jesus is Our Good Shepherd

> *The Lord is my shepherd, I shall not want. He makes me lie down in green pastures; He leads me beside quiet waters. He restores my soul; He guides me in the paths of righteousness*

for His name's sake. Even though I walk through the valley
of the shadow of death, I fear no evil, for You are with me;
Your rod and Your staff, they comfort me. You prepare a table
before me in the presence of my enemies; You have anointed
my head with oil; my cup overflows. Surely goodness and
lovingkindness will follow me all the days of my life, and I
will dwell in the house of the Lord forever. (Psalm 23:1-6)

I have a small rectangular mirror. One side is the mirror and the other side an image of Jesus Christ, our Good Shepherd. I look at it now as I write this. Around Him are a number of grown sheep, and behind Him is a stream. In His right hand he holds a staff, and in His left hand He holds a little lamb.

I learned an interesting truth from the author, Philip Keller, by reading his book, '*A Shepherd Looks at Psalm 23.*' Keller was once a shepherd. In it, he notes that if a particular lamb was prone to wander from the shepherd's care, the shepherd might break the leg of the lamb and then carry it around his neck until the leg healed.

What may sound like cruelty to some was actually a great act of love. Not only would the shepherd bear the weight of the lamb, but that lamb really got to know the shepherd; his voice, his smell, such that when the lamb was ready to carry its own weight, it now stayed near to the Shepherd. Trust me, that little rascals wandering days were over.

Brokenness in a Christian man's life serves much the same purpose.

I once used this mirror as a point of reference in a class I was teaching on Wednesday evenings at my church. I passed the mirror around as I spoke. I shared that I saw myself as that broken little lamb.

After everyone present had the chance to look at the mirror and the image on the other side of it, I told the class that my prayer for each of them was that the Lord wouldn't have to break their leg, or remove it, to get their undivided attention.

You see, in early December of 2016, my left leg was amputated above my knee. Before the amputation, I met with a vascular surgeon. After his prolonged examination of my severely swollen and cool to the touch left leg, foot, and toes, he told me that if my leg wasn't removed soon, I would soon die due to complications. I looked at him and his team and said, "If this will bring glory to God, then I'm all in."

I found a very meaningful quote in John Eldredge's book, *Wild at Heart*. In context, he spoke of soldiers who have been severely wounded in battle. He stated:

To lose a leg is nothing compared to losing heart.

All too often I have allowed the enemy and my own thinking to drag me down. When I watch people walk, I often utter a prayer that they might rejoice for the gift of their mobility. There have been periods of time where I have greatly lamented the loss of my leg and my immobility. I miss hiking and fording streams. I miss surfing and surf fishing, the ability to help others move, and to serve as I have in the past at my church, and on behalf of others. I miss simply the ability to walk from one room to another in my apartment.

It has been a struggle for me to not lose heart - maybe for you, too. As it is with the school of brokenness, I would have never signed up for this. It has been quite an adjustment, to say the least. But my God is faithful. God is faithful! He is faithful and He has a plan and a purpose for me and for you. He has a high call for each of us.

I have a dear friend and brother in Christ, named Daniel. Daniel was born with cerebral palsy and has been in a wheelchair all his life. He has suffered in many ways, but the joy of the Lord is all over this man. Just recently he spoke straight to my heart with these precious words: "It's not my wheelchair that defines me. It's my relationship with God in Christ that defines me."

Yes, I've known suffering and great disappointment, and who among us hasn't? However, I have found that my condition in my wheelchair affords me an even greater opportunity to not only share the love of Jesus Christ with others, but to be a reflection of the One I share about. For this I am so grateful, but I first had to surrender myself and my condition to God - wholesale and whole-heartedly. In warfare, they call it unconditional surrender. God loves me and He is in control. He loves all who call upon His name and He has a role for every Christian man and woman to fulfill.

I believe one of the greatest roles He has for our lives is to serve as a watchmen on the wall.

Our Role as Watchmen

> *"Son of man, I have made you a watchman for the people of Israel; so hear the word I speak and give them warning from me." (Ezekiel 33:7)*

The role of watchman is much like that of a soldier who is serving as point man. God has established His believers to serve as, and to be, watchmen. By the power and presence of the Holy Spirit, we can clearly see the coming danger in the spiritual realm. We must not be silent. We must warn the people about the difficult times that we are living in and that are coming, and inspire them to abandon sin, and turn their hearts towards God.

Our watchman's role is multifaceted. It entails vigilance - that we are to stand on guard, to be on the alert, and to remain on post with our eyes and ears wide open. Jesus asked this of His disciples in the Garden of Gethsemane, but they failed at that time.

> *And He came to the disciples and found them sleeping, and said to Peter, "So, you* men *could not keep watch with Me for one hour? Keep watching and praying that you may not enter into temptation; the spirit is willing, but the flesh is weak."* (Matthew 26:40-41)

Yes, our flesh is weak. As watchmen, we are to remain alert and on guard, and we can only do this by the power of the indwelling presence of the Spirit of God.

Could it be that the role of being a watchman on the wall is foreign to our culture, as it is also somewhat foreign to most churches? All too often, the scope of our view is limited. We are to train ourselves and others what it means to stand and remain on the alert.

The role of a watchman is also not a feeling or an emotionally-driven role. The role of watchman is commanded of all men and women that know, follow, and love our Lord and Risen Savior, Jesus Christ. We are all called to be watchmen, and to watch and pray.

I found an excellent commentary on "The Task of a Watchman" by Dave Butts of Harvest Prayer Ministries I have incorporated a number of his comments in the following.

"What is it we are looking for as we pray? I would suggest that we first look for an enemy attack. Certainly in Old Testament times, this sort of defensive watchfulness was at the heart of the task. The watchman on the wall was always on the alert for any attempt of an enemy to attack or infiltrate the city. Too many times, the walls of the Church and of our cities today are open to attack because of a lack of watchfulness. In 2 Corinthians 2:11, Paul wrote that we are "not unaware" of the schemes of the enemy. Unless praying watchmen are on duty, we too often find ourselves painfully unaware of the attempts of the enemy to disrupt and destroy.

On the opposite end of matters, I believe that the watchmen are also to keep their eyes open to see and discern moves of God. All too often we miss out on what God is doing because we are not paying attention."

A watchman also concerns himself with the needs of others. He serves in a shepherd's manner in this way. A watchman serves in his capacity over his family, over the walls of his home, and his church. A watchman prays for those who do not know Christ - that they might come to Him in faith.

The role of a watchman is not limited to speaking only about the sins and problems of the society, but also includes proclaiming the good news of salvation.

> *How lovely on the mountains are the feet of him who brings good news, who announces peace and brings good news of happiness, who announces salvation,* and *says to Zion, "Your God reigns!" Listen! Your watchmen lift up* their *voices, they shout joyfully together; for they will see with their own eyes when the Lord restores Zion. Break forth, shout joyfully together, you waste places of Jerusalem; for the Lord has comforted His people, He has redeemed Jerusalem. The Lord has bared His holy arm in the sight of all the nations, that all the ends of the earth may see the salvation of our God.* (Isaiah 52:7-10)

Again, in Romans 10:15 it's stated:

> *How will they preach unless they are sent? Just as it is written, "How beautiful are the feet of those who bring good news of good things!" (Romans 10:15)*

Hum, beautiful feet (foot) - I've never thought nor heard that of mine, but I have since changed my mind about this.

A watchman not only proclaims the good news, but he has been personally equipped by God to see what others do not see, and to have the unique capacity to see when, where, and how the enemy is invading. He is to sound the alarm *(blow the trumpet)* at the first sign of enemy movement or presence. A watchman sees human needs much like a shepherd does in his watch over his sheep.

Henry Blackaby, in his message, "The Role of a Spiritual Watchman – Herald of His Coming," says this:

"A spiritual watchman holds in his or her hands life and death. It is as if God has equipped their eyes to see or ears to hear of danger and then has equipped them to know how to blow the horn and to give warning and to call us to pray."

———————————

The nations are in great peril. The judgement of God is coming, and it is ONLY God who decides upon whom that judgment comes, and when.

> *All the nations will be gathered before Him; and He will separate them from one another, as the shepherd separates the sheep from the goats; (Matthew 25:32)*

In chapter 3, I noted that the word, Holy, was one of the only two words used three times in the Word of God. The other is the word, woe *(Rev. 8:13)*. It speaks of the great judgement of God that is to come.

> *Then I looked, and I heard an eagle flying in midheaven, saying with a loud voice, "**Woe, woe, woe** to those who dwell on the earth, because of the remaining blasts of the trumpet of the three angels who are about to sound!" (Revelation 8:13; emphasis mine)*

Merriam-Webster defines the noun, woe, as:

1. a condition of deep suffering from misfortune, affliction, or grief

2. ruinous trouble; calamity; affliction

We are to sound the alarm so as to awaken the sleeping amongst us, as well all those who do not yet know the Lord Jesus Christ. We are to be eyes and ears both of, and for, the church. Indeed, the day of woe is coming to all who dwell on the earth.

> *"Blow a trumpet in Zion, and sound an alarm on My holy mountain! Let all the inhabitants of the land tremble, for the day of the Lord is coming; surely it is near" (Joel 2:1)*

Indeed, this message is a clarion call to all who love the Lord. The word clarion means a strongly expressed demand or request for action. This call is to both Christian men and women who will go out into the world to do the all-important work of evangelizing. We are to reap, to proclaim the good news of Jesus Christ, and to sound the alarm of God's coming judgement.

> *"Do not participate in the unfruitful deeds of darkness, but instead even expose them; for it is disgraceful even to speak of the things which are done by them in secret." (Ephesians 5:11-12)*

We, as a nation, are in a world of hurt. Eternal lives are at stake. To not sound the alarm is akin to a doctor who, after learning that his patient has cancer, chooses not to tell him because he doesn't want to alarm or worry him. In failing to do so, he sentences his patient to death - the doctor is liable. This idea is powerfully stated in the following Scripture, Ezekiel 33:1-7, in regards to our role as a watchman.

> *And the word of the Lord came to me, saying, 2 "Son of man, speak to the sons of your people and say to them, 'If I bring a sword upon a land, and the people of the land take one man from among them and make him their watchman, 3 and he sees the sword coming upon the land and blows on the trumpet and warns the people, 4 then he who hears the sound of the trumpet and does not take warning, and a sword comes and takes him away, his blood will be on his own head. 5 He heard the sound of the trumpet but did not take warning; his blood will be on himself. But had he taken warning, he would have delivered his life. 6 **But if the watchman sees the sword coming and does not blow the trumpet and the people are not warned, and a sword comes and takes a person from them, he is taken away in his iniquity; but his blood I will require from the watchman's hand.**'7 "Now as for you, son of man, I have appointed you a watchman for the house of Israel; so you will*

> *hear a message from My mouth and give them warning from*
> *Me. (Ezekiel 33:1-7, emphasis mine)*

Men, verse 33:6 says should another be lost, we are accountable for not sounding the alarm!

Henry Blackaby continues as he offers the following as a powerful prayer of a watchman:

"Father, we hear You say, 'I have made you a watchman unto your people.' Father, help us to identify Your activity in our life. Help us to feel the weight of giving a warning when the enemy seems to be so active. When Your people are under the strain and the stress, they need to know what it is that has come against them. Lord, You may have given us unusual insight or You are about to because You are about to set us on the walls of our family afresh or our church or our city and You are stirring in our heart. Father, help us to know it is You and to remember that You have done that in other days, and that You will not let this generation go by without many watchmen. You will not let this generation go without warnings so that we can adjust our lives.

"Father, even now You are putting Your hand on many who will make a decision about their life as spiritual watchmen on the walls of Your people or their homes. May You do a great work in our heart, and don't let us ever be afraid to blow the trumpet. So Father, along with the others, I wait for and watch for and expect Your anointing on my life to fulfill such an assignment.

"And You have made me aware of what could happen if they never hear the warning. Enable us in these moments of worship to respond to Your invitation which is so critical for the lives of Your people and our families in the days and months that lie before us. We ask it in the Name of Jesus our Lord."

There is an hour coming, a day of reckoning, when all people will be judged. Darris McNeely, in an article titled 'What Will the Watchman Say?' states the following in this regard:

God warns us through the message of the prophets that sins will demand a day of reckoning. People cannot continue worshipping the false gods of materialism and self, blindly stumbling along in their own righteousness, and expect their affluent standard of living to continue.

God's Word confirms there will be an accounting; the lesson of history is that any people who corrupt their moral core will eventually fade from power.

McNeely closes with the following that he calls '*Warning and Hope:*'

"*This is a time for the watchmen to mount the walls and sound a clear, unmistakable warning message of the dangers facing the world. It is a time to make known the hope of the coming Kingdom of God.*

Isaiah's message stands bright and clear today: "How beautiful upon the mountains are the feet of him who brings good news, who proclaims peace, who brings glad tidings of good things, who proclaims salvation, who says to Zion, 'Your God reigns!' Your watchmen shall lift up their voices, with their voices they shall sing together; for they shall see eye to eye when the Lord brings back Zion" (Isaiah 52:7).

Come, take your place on the walls, work for the Kingdom and pray for its speedy arrival!"

Take Heart

It is said that most wars are won well in advance. This war was won on the cross! The battle we are in has already been won because the battle belongs to the Lord.

> "*that all this assembly may know that the* LORD *does not deliver by sword or by spear; for the battle is the* LORD'S *and He will give you into our hands.*" *(1 Samuel 17:47)*

> *and he said, "Listen, all Judah and the inhabitants of Jerusalem and King Jehoshaphat: thus says the LORD to you, 'Do not fear or be dismayed because of this great multitude, for the battle is not yours but God's. (2 Chronicles 20:15)*

The battle belongs to the Lord.

The Call to Arms!

> *"No weapon that is formed against you will prosper; and every tongue that accuses you in judgment you will condemn. This is the heritage of the servants of the Lord, and their vindication is from Me," declares the Lord. (Isaiah 54:17)*

Brothers and sisters, there's a battle underway and we must not allow ourselves to be blinded to the reality and truth of this. The nations are in peril, and I fear much of the church at large isn't on alert to sound the alarm as it should be sounded - as it must.

> *For what is a man profited if he gains the whole world, and loses or forfeits himself? (Luke 9:25)*

> *Therefore, since Christ has suffered in the flesh, arm yourselves also with the same purpose, because he who has suffered in the flesh has ceased from sin, (1 Peter 4:1)*

The war rages around us, against us, and within us. That old nature wants to rule and reign within us, but it mustn't be given license to do so. We are to die daily to ourselves. The world, the flesh, and the devil compete for our attention. Satan always promises more than he can deliver because, again, he is a liar.

A.W. Tozer, in his book, '*This World: Playground or Battleground,*' states this:

(Worldly) men think of the world, not as a battleground but as a playground. We are not here to fight, we are here to frolic. We are not in a foreign land,

we are at home. We are not getting ready to live, we are already living, and the best we can do is to rid ourselves of our inhibitions and our frustrations and live this life to the full. This, we believe, is a fair summary of the religious philosophy of modern man, openly professed by millions and tacitly held by more multiplied millions who live out that philosophy without having given verbal expression to it.

...A right view of God and the world to come requires that we have also a right view of the world in which we live and our relation to it. So much depends upon this that we cannot afford to be careless about it.

The world is a Battleground, not a playground.

Our minds entertain countless thoughts and emotions daily. Our hearts and minds must be steadfast in Him who is our hope and our Redeemer, Jesus Christ. We must take every thought captive to Christ. We must take hold of His love letter to us, the Word of God, and read it, study it, and meditate upon it in both our personal times of reading and study, and with others who know and love Him and His Word.

God speaks to us most clearly through His Word. We must saturate our minds with the Bible. In doing so, we will hear clearly the commands of our loving and all powerful Most High Commander, God.

We must be ever vigilant and alert to the moves and schemes of the enemy, the devil. He is working overtime in this world. He knows his time is limited and he wants all the company he can gather to spend an eternity with him in hell.

> *For you are all sons of God through faith in Christ Jesus. (Galatians 3:26)*

How wondrous it is to be called a child of the King.

We must sound the alarm. Again, eternity stands in the balance. There are many who do not know the Lord – may we speak the beauty and truth of Him to all we encounter.

Know this, as watchmen on the wall, there is a bull's eye on each of us – front and back. A watchman for the Lord is a desired target of Satan's. Being a watchman puts us in the forefront and makes us a target of the evil one - it puts us dead center on Satan's radar. Again, he identifies each of us as foe!

My brother, this Arise chapter could have as easily been titled, *"Get back in the Saddle!"* If this speaks to you, I offer the following prayer.

"Lord, I don't know if I was thrown off the saddle a while back and just failed to remount, or if I simply got off the horse because the ride was a rough one at the time. Father, hear my prayer. This day I am re-enlisting myself into Your service – for my good and Your Glory! Amen."

I offer the following that re-enlistment entails on our part:

- repentance of our wayward ways
- a wholesale return to the daily reading of the Bible
- to reflect upon and study what it is that we have read
- faithful church attendance, at a fellowship where the Word of God is taught and spoken
- time with other believers
- making ourselves available in service to the church and to those in need
- letting go of all we once held dear to us
- embracing the role of a watchman on the wall
- consistent time in prayer and praise to our Great Commander, Almighty God

Remain on Alert

This is a necessary restatement - a battle rages all around us, and we are each called into this spiritual war. The enemy wants to reclaim the previously occupied territory within us, and he wants to drag countless many with him to his eternal destination - hell.

This is a battle not only for the hearts, minds, and souls of men and women who love Jesus Christ, but also for the hearts, minds, souls of men and women who have yet to embrace the love and saving grace of Jesus Christ.

To My Unbelieving Friends

No doubt, not every man or woman that might read this book is a born-again believer. I graciously pose to those of you who do not yet know Jesus Christ, that you can receive Him right now.

As you've read the many Scriptures in this book, surely the Spirit of God has spoken to you. God loves you and wants fellowship with you. But He is a Holy God - our sins separate us from Him. From eternity past, God purposed that Jesus Christ would come to earth as a man, fully God and fully man, and to live a sinless life. That He would be condemned to death, death on a cross. He gave His life for us on the cross and on the third day, He rose from the grave. We are asked only to believe this about Him, to repent of our old ways, and to trust fully in Jesus Christ.

You see, your eternity lies in the balance.

My friend, open the door to your heart and invite Jesus in.

> *"…if you confess with your mouth Jesus as Lord, and believe in your heart that God raised Him from the dead, you will be saved; for with the heart a person believes, resulting in righteousness, and with the mouth he confesses, resulting in salvation." (Romans 10:9-10)*

Prayer is talking with God. He knows your heart, so don't worry about getting your words just right. Here is a suggested prayer to guide you:

"Lord Jesus, I want to know you personally. I repent of my sins and I thank you for dying on the cross for me. I open the door of my life and receive you as my Savior and Lord. Thank you for forgiving me of my sins and giving me eternal life. Take control of my life. Make me the kind of person You want me to be."

I celebrate with any of you that made a decision for Jesus Christ. If you did so:

- Share your decision with others
- Find a church that teaches the Word of God and attend it
- Get to know your Savior, Jesus Christ

I encourage you to read the book of John in the New Testament. See who He is and who He claims to be.

Get to know Jesus!

> *The seventy returned with joy, saying, "Lord, even the demons are subject to us in Your name." And He said to them, "I was watching Satan fall from heaven like lightning. Behold, I have given you authority to tread on serpents and scorpions, and over all the power of the enemy, and nothing will injure you. Nevertheless do not rejoice in this, that the spirits are subject to you, but rejoice that your names are recorded in heaven." (Luke 10:17-20)*

Make sure your name is recorded in heaven.

The Coming Return of Jesus Christ

The many fronts in this battle will only continue to enlarge and expand as we draw nearer to the glorious and imminent return of Jesus Christ. Likely you've heard it said, "What one generation rejects or abhors, the next generation will embrace." We see just that all around us today. There is such evil and confusion in the world today, just like in the days of Noah.

Indeed, things are changing in the world. We are currently living in an age where these vices and others are becoming more commonplace, even embraced. Amongst these alarming concerns and trends are:

- The Christian faith is no longer considered a virtue, but faith in anything else is wonderfully received, even celebrated.
- Marriage is becoming obsolete in the eyes of many young people.
- The incorporation of artificial intelligence (AI) in nearly all of our electronic communications and browsing history, online shopping habits, etc. point to the coming one world religion.
- Young people are trying on various forms of transgender as if it was little more than a fashion statement, and they become all the more popular for it.
- Sexual promiscuity continues to escalate, especially in its more deviate forms.
- Satan worship is skyrocketing.
- The continuing rise and force of the alternative lifestyle advocates - alternative anything.

We must sound the alarm.

> *For the coming of the Son of Man will be just like the days of Noah. For as in those days before the flood they were eating and drinking, marrying and giving in marriage, until the day that Noah entered the ark, and they did not understand until the flood came and took them all away; so will the coming of the Son of Man be. (Matthew 24:37-39)*

It is, indeed, as if in the days of Noah. The signs are all around us.

Men, the church of Jesus Christ, the body of believers who will one day be His bride, needs vigilant and alert watchmen on the walls, and on their knees - on our knees. We are to call out to those around us about what we see in our midst, and sound the alarm to warn people about what is presently here, and what is coming.

> *And He [Jesus] was also saying to the crowds, "When you see a cloud rising in the west, immediately you say, 'A shower is coming,' and so it turns out. And when you see a south wind blowing, you say, 'It will be a hot day,' and it turns out that way. You hypocrites! You know how to analyze the appearance of the earth and the sky, but why do you not analyze [discern] this present time? (Luke 12:54-56)*

In Closing

My brothers and sisters in Christ, we must awaken and discern this present time. Yes, a war rages - it truly is a battle for the hearts, minds, and souls of men and women - Christian and non-Christian alike. Nature declares this – time is running out. Times of great persecution are happening around the world, and we shouldn't be surprised when such times come to our shores.

We must be ever on the alert, we must stand firm in the faith, we must be strong in the Lord and in the power of His might, and we must act like men and women of God.

Are you ready for battle?

Study Guide - Chapter 6

Day 1

a) Look back at your life and think about that time, that moment, when you first gave your heart and life to Jesus Christ. To the best of your recollection, describe that moment - put a date, place, and time to it if you are able.

b) Have you lost or left your first love for Him since then? Take a prayerful moment and consider the things that likely have robbed you of that first love. Be honest with yourself and with the Lord.

c) What areas of your past life continue to draw you away from the Lord?

d) When old, hurtful or painful memories or recollections come to mind, how do you respond?

e) What changes to your initial responses can you make in the future?

Responses:

Day 2

a) Has there been a re-enlistment moment in your life in the past - a moment when you recognized that you had grown distant from the Lord? Maybe it was a rededication or just the fact that you knew you hadn't been walking faithfully with the Lord.

b) If so, how did you respond then?

c) How might you respond now?

Responses:

Day 3

a) In reference to the passages in Matthew 16:13-16, answer the question Jesus asked of His disciples and us when He asked: "Who do you say that I am?"

b) How might you go about asking this question of others in your acquaintance or in your day to day life? Again, all of eternity rests on one's answer.

c) Read through the New Testament book of John and identify several of the claims He makes about Himself. Look for the seven 'I am' statements Jesus made therein.

Responses:

d) Regarding your role as a watchman on the wall, what do you sense the Lord is asking of you in this capacity?

e) At this present time in your life, what challenges are you facing that might want to turn you aside or away from this role?

f) How might you better respond?

Responses:

Day 4

a) Do you want to make a rededication to the Lord; are you ready to re-enlist?

b) Pen a prayer to the Lord. Confess your love and need for Him. In your own words, tell Him you're ready to 'saddle up' again.

c) What might you foresee as a couple of the first things you must be about in your re-enlistment?

Responses:

<u>Day 5</u>

a) Each of the following Scripture passages speak of being a watchman. Read each and comment about how it speaks to you about being a watchman.
b) What direction and/or encouragement does each offer?

Passage: *Beloved, do not believe every spirit, but test the spirits to see whether they are from God, because many false prophets have gone out into the world. (1 John 4:1)*

<u>Response:</u>

Passage: *"But you, be sober in all things, endure hardship, do the work of an evangelist, fulfill your ministry." (2 Timothy 4:5)*

<u>Response:</u>

Passage: *"The end of all things is near; therefore, be of sound judgment and sober spirit for the purpose of prayer." (1 Peter 4:7)*

<u>Response:</u>

Passage: *"Devote yourselves to prayer, keeping alert in it with an attitude of thanksgiving;" (Colossians 4:2)*

<u>Response:</u>

Passage: *On your walls, O Jerusalem, I have appointed watchmen; all day and all night they will never keep silent. You who make mention of the Lord, take no rest for yourselves; (Isaiah 62:6)*

Response:

Passage: *But if the watchman sees the sword coming and does not blow the trumpet and the people are not warned, and a sword comes and takes a person from them, he is taken away in his iniquity; but his blood I will require from the watchman's hand.' (Ezekiel 33:6)*

Response:

Bibliography

Chapter 1

Orwell, George. *1984:* New York: Penguin, 1949.

Anderson, Neil, *Walking Through the Darkness:* Here's Life Publishers, 1991.

Chapter 2

Frangipane, Francis, *The Three Battlegrounds*: New Wine Press, 2006.

Nouwen, Henri, J.M., *The Wounded Healer*: Random House, 1979.

Edwards, Gene, *The Tales of Three Kings*: Christian Books, 1980.

Chapter 4

Anderson, Lisa, *The Dating Manifesto*: David C. Cook, 2015.

Tozer, A. W., *The Pursuit of God*: Camp Hill, Pa.: Christian Publications, 1993.

Chapter 5

Spangler, Ann, *The Names of God*: Zondervan, Feb 22, 2011.

Tozer, A. W., *The Pursuit of God*: Camp Hill, Pa.: Christian Publications, 1993.

Chapter 6

Keller, W P., *A Shepherd Looks at Psalm 23*: Zondervan, 1970.

Eldredge, John, *Wild at Heart*: Thomas Nelson, 2001.

Tozer, A. W., *This World: Playground or Battleground*: Moody Publishers, 2009.

End Notes

Chapter 1

Anderson, Tonilee and Brooks, Bobbye (September 19, 2007). *Spiritual Warfare: Understanding the Battle.* Posted by Bible Study Tools; retrieved from https://www.biblestudytools.com/bible-study/topical-studies/spiritual-warfare-lesson-1-understanding-the-battle-11554631.html

Chapter 3

Thomas, Susan (August 11, 2011). *Is My Problem My Thought Life?* Posted by Association of Christian Counseling; retrieved from https://christiancounseling.com/blog/uncategorized/is-my-problem-my-thought-life/

Chapter 4

Sproul, R.C. (posting date not given). *Standing firm in the Faith.* Retrieved from https://www.ligonier.org/learn/devotionals/standing-firm-in-the-lord/

Boekestein, William - blogger for Ligonier Ministries (May 22, 2013). *Husbands, 8 Admonitions to Love Your Wife.* Retrieved from URL: https://www.ligonier.org/blog/husbands-8-admonitions-love-your-wife/

Kennebrew, Dr. Delesslyn, A. (2012). *What is True Worship?* Retrieved from: https://www.christianitytoday.com/biblestudies/bible-answers/spirituallife/what-is-true-worship.html

Chapter 5

Got Questions Organization post (posting date not given). *What does selah mean in the Bible?* Retrieved from https://www.gotquestions.org/selah.html

McDowell, Josh (January 1, 2017). *Attributes of God.* Retrieved from **(may delete this)** https://www.josh.org/resources/spiritual-growth/attributes-of-god/

Sala, Dr. Harold J. (September 3, 2018). *How Do I Hear the Voice of God?* Retrieved from https://www.guidelines.org/devotional/how-do-i-hear-the-voice-of-god/

Chapter 6

Rogers, Adrian (August 22, 2018). *Two Days That Will Steal Your Joy.* Retrieved from

https://www.crosswalk.com/devotionals/loveworthfinding/love-worth-finding-august-22-2018.html

Butts, Dave (posting date not given). *The Task of a Watchman.* Retrieved from https://www.harvestprayer.com/resources/personal-2/task-of-watchman/

Blackaby, Henry (October 2007). *The Role of a Spiritual Watchman – Herald of His Coming (A Family Watchman).* Retrieved from http://www.heraldofhiscoming.com/Past%20Issues/2007/October/the_role_of_a_spiritual_watchman.htm

McNeely (July 28, 2007). *What Will the Watchman Say?* Retrieved from https://www.ucg.org/the-good-news/the-role-of-a-watchman-part-2-who-are-todays-watchmen

Throughout this book

Printed in the United States
By Bookmasters